JIM CROW DID NOT EXIST IN MY BACKYARD

by
JOSEPH M MOORE

Jim Crow Did Not Exist in my Backyard

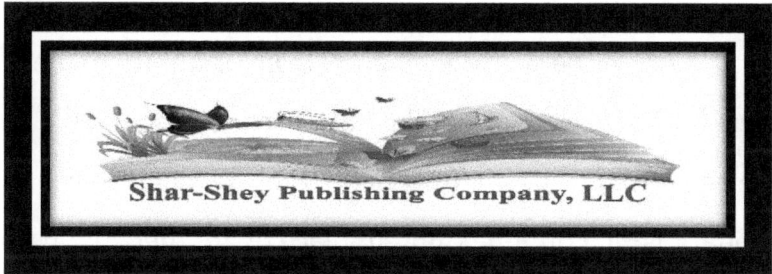

Shar-Shey Publishing Company, LLC

P.O. Box 841
Tobyhanna, PA 18466
(973) 348-5067

Copyright © 2016 Joseph M. Moore
ISBN: 13: 978-0-9972668-6-3
ISBN: 10: 0-9972668-6-4
Publisher: Shar-Shey Publishing Company LLC
Book Cover Designed by: Dynastys CoverMe
Edited by: Latarsha Banks

[1]

Preface

All of the world's scholars from antiquity to the present have argued that the only constant in the universe is change. Change, as defined by Webster's Dictionary is "To put one thing in place of another." I, on the other hand, take issue with that definition when it comes to racism. Racism does not change; it evolves, and its evolution can be traced all the way back to a point when man noticed the rainbow of colors associated with the human species and how they interact within their social, political, and economic condition within society. Racism is always self-centered and self-serving, and I believe the concept of self, entered man's psyche the moment he became aware of his racial identity by the teachings of their family. I am white, and that is good; he is black, and that is bad.

Jim Crow Did Not Exist in my Backyard

During the decade of the 1950's segregation and Jim Crow laws were so interwoven into Southern society that they became a way of life. Unfortunately, African Americans were the recipients of these biased laws. Of all the racist laws enacted beginning at the end of the Civil War to the mid-1960's, voter suppression, intimidation and downright voter nullification were common tactics employed to disenfranchise the black citizens of the South. Nevertheless, they still showed up at the polls to vote. Murder, lynchings, and beatings were other methods used, yet they still showed up to vote. However, the most effective tactic employed by the peace-loving white citizens of the South were the Poll Tax and Literacy Test.

Originally, literacy tests were not designed to eliminate Blacks from the voting booth. They were designed to keep Irish-American Catholics from voting in the North. In 1855 Connecticut became the first state to enact such a law, and in 1857 Massachusetts followed suit.

After the tremendous bloodbath and deaths of hundreds of thousands of soldiers during the Civil War and during Reconstruction the states ratified the 15th amendment to the US constitution on February 3, 1870. It states, "The right of a citizen to vote shall not be denied by the United States or by any state because race, color, or previous condition of servitude." This amendment created a huge problem for all the Southern states and numerous other states throughout the country. In many counties throughout the South, blacks outnumbered their white counterparts by a margin of two to one. Something had to be done to maintain the social, economic and political structure of the White South.

In 1889, Florida along with ten other Southern states adopted the Poll Tax. In Mississippi, the Poll Tax and literacy test were enacted. Those two measures worked exceedingly well; so well, in fact, it took almost one hundred years to declare those measures unconstitutional. Some examples of the questions being asked of African Americans who, for the most part, were rural, uneducated farmers were, A. "If a person charged with treason denies his guilt, how many persons must testify against him before he can be convicted?" B. "In what year did congress gain the right to prohibit the migration of persons from other states?"

It must be emphasized that the vast majority of people taking the test were poor rural farmers with little or no formal education. Most did not read or write. However, if by some miracle they were able to answer the questions correctly, they were then asked to interpret the meaning of the question. If the black voter applicant was successful in meeting all the requirements for voting, their next obstacle to overcome was not being lynched to death for attempting to vote in the first place.

Most whites in the South who lived on farms or in rural areas could not read or afford to pay the poll tax in order to register to vote. However, the state made an exception for those whites who happened to be in the same situation as their black counterparts. That exception was known as the Grandfather Clause. It allowed for the grandchildren of those people who could vote before 1870 to have the right to vote without paying the poll tax or taking the literacy test. African Americans could not claim that exemption. The poll tax and literacy test were made illegal with the passage of the Voting Rights Act of 1965.

The economic and political power of Africans Americans as compared to White Americans was nonexistent during the decades of the fifties and sixties. Discrimination in everything against blacks was strictly enforced in the South in general and New Orleans. The only jobs open to blacks without fear of discrimination were dishwashers, janitors, domestics, waiters, and housekeepers. There was no Equal Employment Opportunity Commission (EEOC) at that time.

As a child during this period, economics and other political issues were of little concern to me. However, as I look back, the neighborhood in which I lived in was a wonderful place.

Yes, the boot of segregation and racism was on the throat of our neighborhood. Yes, city services were separate and unequal. Whites got the best and colored people got the leftovers. But in spite of all of that my neighborhood was clean and well kept. All of the homes were single or double family homes. As far as I could tell all of the families were headed by working fathers and most mothers were stay-at-home moms.

My mother, Mrs. Leona Bryant Moore, was one of four licensed hair stylists in the neighborhood. My father, Mr. Joseph M. Moore, was an independent businessman. He was one of two icemen in the neighborhood. This was the era of ice-boxes, not refrigerators, although iceboxes were quickly becoming a thing of the past. The ice would be placed in a separate compartment in the ice box in order to keep items cool and prevent them from spoiling too soon. It was low-tech and inefficient, but it accomplished what it was designed to do.

During those long hot summer days in New Orleans, I can remember my father coming home from a hard day's work, parking his truck, a 1948 International, alongside the house and begin to wind down. As soon as my father would park his truck, my friends and I would descend upon it. We would climb upon the truck bed get under the tarpaulin, a waterproof canvas, gather ice chips and eat them. Plus, being under the tarpaulin gave the impression of being in an air-conditioned room. Although I only spent a short time with my father, ten years before he passed, The Lord blessed me by giving me a vivid memory of my time spent with him.

I never referred to my father as dad or daddy; I only referred to him as Honey. I thought that was his name because that was all I ever heard my mother call him. Honey was the de facto neighborhood recreation superintendent. Along with other parents, he made sure that the kids in the neighborhood, including my white friends, had something to do during the summer. Sometimes my white friends would join us in our cool sanctuary. Back then we knew that black children and white children could not socialize in public, like going to the movies together or playing together in the segregated city parks. But our neighborhood was different.

My neighborhood was a segregated yet integrated of sorts. On some streets, there were black families, and on others, there were white families, yet our backyards were interconnected separated by fences. As I recall, we all lived in peace. I cannot think of a single instance where there were any racial problems. Because of the type of work my father was engaged in and the fact that he was constantly in the homes of white families, I believe his interaction with those families contributed to peaceful coexistence. Plus, having the ability to pass for white could not hurt. At Christmas time my father would come home with gifts given to him by white families. In turn, some of those families would not have the money to pay my father for ice. Therefore he would give it to them, or he would tell them to pay him when they could. Those and other acts of kindness prevented hostilities and promoted peaceful coexistence.

Jim Crow Did Not Exist in my Backyard

As previously stated, our backyards were separated by fences and those very same fences were our playground equipment. We would climb them, play on top of them and we would walk on top of them as if walking on a tightrope. Sometimes my mother would bake T-cakes, and the aroma would spread all over the neighborhood, making my house a magnet for all my friends. At other times my friends' moms would do the same thing with the same results. God, I loved my mother and father. I just was not allowed enough time to spend with them. I get so angry to see and hear of children mistreating their parents. If they only knew what it meant to lose them.

The restrictions of racism and Jim Crow laws in most Southern cities were complete and unforgiving. New Orleans was, for the most part, different in terms of association. In the cities of Mississippi, Alabama and others, black and white families were so isolated they never got to know each other in a non-confrontational context. Other than master-servant relationships, contact was very limited, allowing for hostilities to reside just under the surface. Black adults and children were not allowed in white neighborhoods after the sun went down without a good reason for being there. In New Orleans in some instances, however, we were allowed in white neighborhoods, and whites came to ours. This was due to Mardi Gras and the Eureka Brass Band, an all negro marching band which paraded during Carnival time and the St. Charles Avenue streetcar. In New Orleans, the streetcar was an electric vehicle which ran on tracks. The streetcar stop was located approximately six blocks from my house. In order for us to reach the stop, we had to walk through the white neighborhood. Sometimes whites had to enter our neighborhood in order to catch the closest city bus. This interaction allowed us in a small way to get to know each other, especially the kids.

I do not know if the city authorities realized their restrictions on us with regard to the city's own playgrounds and parks had little to no effect. The levees, our streets, and backyards became our parks. What we did not have we did not miss, plus our backyard fences became our playground equipment allowing us to reach all the fruit and nuts which grew back there.

In my neighborhood, there were many different species of trees everywhere. My house was located on Hickory street in the Carrolton section of the city. In my front yard, there was a huge oak tree. It was so large its shade was cast over the entire intersection. As kids, the majesty of that tree was inspiring.

Jim Crow Did Not Exist in my Backyard

If any one of us saw someone abusing the tree, we would put a stop to it or alert our parents.

In the evening when play time was over, and the neighborhood settled down into its pleasant Southern night, we would gather on my front porch under my big oak tree to tell or listen to stories. Listening to some of the stories some of my friends told made me wonder if we lived on the same planet, especially some of the stories my white friends told. Yet there was an upside, as we told our stories our diction and the use of the English language steadily improved thanks to our parents. Education was taken very serious in our families. To the best of my recollection, all my friends graduated from high school, and most went on to college including me.

As the sweet smell of magnolia trees permeated the night air, our parents and grandparents would sometimes join us. When my grandmother began to speak, all of the children gathered there would become silent. She would begin by relating when she was a child still living on the master's plantation as a sharecropper. As my grandmother related her stories of how black people suffered under segregation and Jim Crow, we began to realize as we listened that it was up to us to pass on her stories to the next generation. Sadly, many African

American children and their parents have lost the narrative of their history.

Most black people of that time lived on the same plantation their parents lived on as slaves, and they lived under the same harsh and brutal conditions of slavery only not in name.

After reconstruction, most of the master's land which was divided up among the ex-slaves (40 acres and a mule) reverted back to the masters whereby forcing the ex-slaves to remain on the plantation because there was no other place for them to go.

During my youth, New Orleans was no different than any other Southern city as it relates to segregation. From schools, both public and private to public policy, Jim Crow was the law of the land except in my back yard. When my friends and I got together, the color of our skin vanished. Mainly on weekends and during the summer, my backyard and that of my neighbors became one of our many playgrounds. Although many of my white friends enjoyed all the rights and privileges afforded them by the racist city authorities, they rarely visited the city parks. There was no need.

On January 1, 1863, by executive order of President Abraham Lincoln, the Emancipation Proclamation was issued.

Jim Crow Did Not Exist in my Backyard

Most people think this proclamation outlawed slavery and freed all the slaves, but it did neither. Slavery remained legal in those Southern states which remained loyal to the union and freed those slaves who were in active rebellion against the union. The 13th amendment to the US Constitution did what the Emancipation Proclamation did not do.

According to my grandmother, at the end of Reconstruction, the South had positioned itself to regain its political, social and economic power it lost during the Civil War. The catchphrase was "The south will rise again." To some extent it did. Once the Southern democrats took over the US House, Senate, and the Judiciary, Jim Crow was born. Most of the land divided among the ex-slaves reverted back to the masters. The new African Americans were put in an untenable position: either remain on the old master's plantation as a neo-slave or be removed from the plantation and out on the street. Being out on the street was not a place a black person wanted to be in those small Southern towns. They could have been arrested, placed on the chain gang or, worst of all, be hung from a tree which was a common occurrence at that time.

As I listened to her, I knew she was directing her stories to the children sitting around her.

She knew we were the next generation to pass her stories on. But, at that time we had more important things on our minds like riding our bicycles, playing with my dog Blackie or generally, just having fun with our friends. But we listened intently, and I never forgot her stories.

During the 1950s and 1960s, everything was proclaimed to be separate but equal, but we knew better. As an example, some of the textbooks my school would receive from the Board of Education would be stamped with the name of a white school. Be that as it may have been, we worked with what we had and changed those things when we could. But, when it came to my backyard and that of my friends, there was no such thing as separate but equal. Everything was equal. Although we had no official playground equipment to speak of, what we did have was our imagination and a way to make what we imagined a reality. That is the power of childhood.

My backyard was divided into three sections. Although I had a front yard where my big oak tree resided, most of the fun took place in the backyard. The first, or side section, was located between my house and that of my neighbor's house. A six-foot wooden fence divided the front yard from the side yard. Anyone who has gone through basic military training

Jim Crow Did Not Exist in my Backyard

knows what we used the fence for, and I am here to declare that white men or, in our case, white boys can jump. The second or middle section of my backyard was the place where my mother hung out the laundry. Also, during the summer my father would build the swimming pool in this section of the yard. There were two structures located there. A two-car garage and a small shed used to store bundles of newspapers which I sold to the trash man for five cents a pound.

The two structures were also used as pseudo-playground equipment. We would run up and down the roofs and jump from building to building without any of us falling off. The third section of the yard was an area where my father planted a small garden and sugarcane patch. It was also an area where my fig and pecan trees grew. Needless to say, we kids were always in that section of the yard when the pool was not up.

In my childhood, there was another playmate in our circle we all adored, and that was my dog, Blackie. The kids in the neighborhood did not look upon Blackie as a big black dog.

He was looked upon as another friend and playmate. I was about five when my father got Blackie for me. To this day I can still see him running toward me and jumping into my arms. I wish all my days were filled with such happiness and joy as I travel my life journey.

When my father and I brought Blackie home, everybody including my cat fell in love with him. You might say Blackie became the neighborhood dog. He was welcome in all my friends' backyards. Blackie was always included in our play; he just seemed to fit in so well.

There were two structures in this area of my backyard. A small storage shed where my father and I bundled old newspapers for sale. Approximately once a week, a man driving a horse-drawn cart would come into the neighborhood and buy the bundled newspapers for five cents a pound. During that time period, horse-drawn carts were not an uncommon sight in most neighborhoods. On a daily basis, a man would drive his horse-drawn cart around the neighborhoods selling fresh fruit and vegetables. Life was much simpler then.

The other structure was the garage. It was much larger than the shed, and they were located next to each other. Access to the roof of each structure was easy and simple, so much so that we would run and jump from roof to roof never considering the danger of falling off. The roof of the shed was five feet high at its lowest point whereby it became our launching point

Jim Crow Did Not Exist in my Backyard

when we were attempting to fly.

On this one particular afternoon, my mother was in the kitchen baking T-cakes. Those were the best cookies I have ever tasted in my life, and my friends can attest to that. The smell of those baking cakes permeated throughout the neighborhood as I would sit on the roof of the shed along with my friend Elmon. Minutes later our white friend Tommy joined us. He was wearing a large towel tied around his neck with an "S" drawn on the back. He was a huge Superman fan. We did not pay much attention to him; we'd seen him dressed like that before. As we sat there, Tommy stood up saying he could jump off the roof and fly like Superman. When we told, him he couldn't he stood up and jumped off the roof. Fear had not become a part of our lives at that time. Well, needless to say, he did not fly, but his cape did wave in the wind. When he landed, Blackie was there to lick his face making him feel like he really did fly. As he stood up, he said, "Did you guys see that I was flying."

We look down at him saying, "Yeah, right."

Tommy rejoined us on the roof when a thought came into my mind. I stood up, jumped off and ran into my house. A few minutes later I returned wearing my Hop-along Cassidy

Western outfit with six shooters and a ten-gallon hat. Hopalong Cassidy was my hero. I rejoined my friends on the roof, at which time I told my friend Elmon to go down and place Blackie under the edge of the roof and hold him there until I said to let him go. I walked to the edge of the roof and looked down. Blackie was in position and standing very still as I motioned to Elmon to move. Tommy stood at the edge of the roof next to me; he knew what I was up to. I was going to attempt one of my all-time favorite Hopalong Cassidy moves by jumping on the back of my dog-horse from a second-floor balcony.

Right at the moment of my leap, Blackie looked up at me, and I guess he decided that I was not going to jump off the roof onto his back today and moved forward. I missed his back and landed on my butt. We begin to laugh as my mother brought out the tea cakes onto the back porch. We ate them to our heart's delight.

The anticipation of summer and school closing excited us especially after emerging from what we thought was a long, cold winter. Vacation time offered us the opportunity to explore and develop within our community in spite of being denied basic human rights. However, just because summer vacation was in full swing did not mean that our education and studies were on vacation too. The Black church took up where school left off.

Religion, education, and the humanities were key elements in the development of our body, mind, and soul of all the children in the neighborhood. Notwithstanding the fact that we were taught very little about our culture and heritage in school, Black church became our reference point regarding our past and the Black press became our reference point for current events. The seeds of the civil rights movement were being planted in our minds.

Our parents played an important role in our education and development as tolerant human beings. We were taught to love and respect our fellow human beings, to acquire as much knowledge about the world in which we live and to love God with all our mind, body, and soul. To all the parents in the neighborhood, reading comprehension was the key for the world to become our oyster. Therefore, the Black church was a vital component of life in my community. The church was a place where we welcomed new life into the world and buried the life which departed from it. In between those two events, the foundation of our existence was being molded.

Joseph M. Moore

As a child, I considered myself very lucky because, unlike others, I had two pathways to God. I was baptized Catholic, plus I attended Catholic schools, and I was an altar boy. On the other side of the coin, my mother father and grandparents were Baptist with my grandfather, The Rev. Joseph Henry Bryant, being a Baptist minister. Due to the fact that God was the center of our universe, there were no conflicts in my household as it related to church affiliation. We all served the same God regardless of how He was being served. I was taught this as a child, and I still believe it to this day.

On Sundays after early morning mass, I would return home, eat breakfast with my family and then prepare to attend Sunday School. Morning Star Baptist Church was our neighborhood church and part-time school. At the completion of Sunday School, my friends and I would return home, change out of our Sunday best and prepare for a full day of fun and adventure. My White friends did not attend church with us; they attended their own church. However, in the afternoon we would meet up in someone's backyard, climb our fig tree and eat the fruit it bore or meet up behind the church to gather pecans. At bedtime, we would say our prayers thanking God for the many blessings He bestowed upon us earlier that day.

Vacation Bible school was just that, a school; only it dealt with religious subjects.

Although religion was the main subject, reading, writing, and arithmetic were other key elements in order to be successful in Bible school. Bible school, to the best of my knowledge, was held between June and July on Saturday evenings between six and seven in the church sanctuary. The students ranged in age from approximately five to teenagers.

Once we gathered inside the church, we were divided into groups by age. Parents took an active part in our religious education. Having a Bible was mandatory. After gathering into our respective groups, we were taught lessons from the Bible which included reading and explaining what we had just read. For a youngster, being able to read and comprehend was a must. Our instructors made sure we accomplished that task.

At the conclusion of that portion of our studies, the fun really began. We were divided into groups of six by age and were led to the pulpit area of the church. Normally, each group had between six and eight members. At this point, the moderator would further divide us into equal numbers and place us opposite of each other with our Bibles at our sides. The moderator would call us to attention and say "draw swords" whereby we would raise our Bibles to waste level and wait for further instructions. Next, the moderator would announce a bible verse: *"Matthew chapter 5 verse 8"*. We would then open our Bibles and search for that chapter and verse. The first person to find and read verbatim that chapter and verse won points for his or her team. The team with the most points in their age group won. At the conclusion of Vacation Bible School, the members of each winning team would receive a new Bible and be publicly recognized at the conclusion of Sunday church services.

Vacation Bible School opened in all African American churches in New Orleans during the summer. I don't know if this was true with White churches. I had no idea of the goings on in their churches. To be honest, with the exception of the Catholic Church, I do not know what goes on in their churches to this day. All of the activities which took place in our neighborhood during the summer had a positive effect on our community for Black and White kids. You might say we were in school year-round, and it paid off.

Race relations during the 50's and 60's were an abstract

term in my neighborhood as it related to all the kids. Actually, prior to the birth of the Civil Rights Movement, we had no idea of what we were being denied. Our parents, however, did. As a child, I did not feel like I was being denied anything. This was due to the fact that my parents supplied all my needs. We knew we could not go where White people went, and we didn't care because being with them or not, did not distract from what we were doing as kids. Adults should pay close attention to their children's innocence and learn from it. When I would play with my White friends, all I saw was another kid whose skin color was just a little lighter than mine. My world and that of the White community co-existed but did not mingle, with the exception of my backyard.

My neighborhood was self-contained. Other than having to go to the hospital or having to take care of business elsewhere from time to time, there was really no reason to leave it. Our school was approximately one block from most of our homes. This is why many Black parents opposed bussing their children long distances to White schools to achieve integration. There was four grocery stores and a butcher's shop within walking distance.

For entertainment, there were nightclubs which catered

only to Black people and a segregated movie theater within four blocks from my home. As I mentioned, this was the era of horse-drawn carts patrolling the neighborhoods selling wares. Not only did they sell fruits and vegetables, but they also sold pots and pans at a reasonable price. The men operating those carts were both Black and White.

The high point of our weekend was Saturday afternoon, movie day. The Roxy Theater was within walking distance from our homes. It was one of those Jim Crow theaters where Black folks had to march up two flights of stairs on the outside, rain or shine, to enter the building to our seating area. We did not care; all we wanted to do was get in and have fun. Naturally, the entrance for Whites was at ground level. Unlike the movie theaters of today which only show a feature presentation, back in those days, we were shown a cartoon, a series, a second feature, and a feature presentation. One of the first movies I saw at the Roxy was Bud Abbott, and Lou Costello meet Frankenstein Dracula and the Wolfman. As the movie was being shown, kids would scream and yell throughout the theater. At the conclusion of the movies, we would leave the theater and go our separate ways. Later that evening we would meet in someone's backyard, sit around the fruit tree eat fruit and discuss and act out what we had saw earlier that day.

Jim Crow segregation laws were designed to separate Black citizens from White citizens in all things. As a by-product of those laws, African Americans were degraded and humiliated as second-class citizens. An example of this was the Jim Crow restaurant and the services they provided. These were White-owned restaurants and sandwich shops, for whites only in my community. If we wanted to place an order, we had to go to the rear of the restaurant where the garbage and trash were stored and place our order at the back door or through a small window built into the wall. Once our order was delivered, we could eat our sandwiches in the rear as long as we stayed out of sight. But, it was not all bad back there. We had a few perks. Sometimes the black cooks would see us back there and bring out extra fries and sodas, for free.

In the pseudo-integrated community in which I lived, Black and White families rarely came in contact with each other and never socialized, although my parents knew most of them. The only white adults I recall coming into my home were those trying to sell us something. On the other hand, when they ran out of ice their children would be sent to my home to inquire whether or not my father had any leftover ice and, if so, could he deliver it. Of course, my father would oblige. Yet, as we walked around the neighborhood, we did exchange pleasantries to greet each other by saying good morning or good afternoon.

To the best of my recollection, there was never any racial strife in my neighborhood and only minor incidents in the city as compared to other Southern cities. In Mississippi, Alabama, and other Southern states it seemed as if they were trying to recreate the Civil War. Yet the city of New Orleans was quiet, for the most part. Throughout my adult life, I have wondered why New Orleans never underwent a major Civil Rights disturbance. It was no different from any other city in the Deep South and just as segregated. Yet there was something different and unique about New Orleans. The African American community was not completely in the dark as to what was going on throughout the South. There were bombings, lynchings, and murders of Black people in many Southern States, yet, to the best of my knowledge, none of those horrible crimes were committed in New Orleans. Why?

If someone living in Paris France, Madrid, Spain or Johannesburg, South Africa were asked, "Have you ever heard of Jackson, Mississippi or Birmingham, Alabama or Little Rock,

Jim Crow Did Not Exist in my Backyard

Arkansas," the probable answer would be no. However, if
those same people were asked if they had ever heard of New
Orleans, more than likely the answer would be yes.

In my opinion, segregation in New Orleans seemed to
have had a softer side as compared to other Southern cities. It
had to be perception, in most cases, the perception was more
important than reality. In the case of New Orleans, this is very
true. At least once a year New Orleans is placed on the world's
stage, and the world comes to New Orleans in order to share in
the good times of Mardi Gras and spend millions of tourist dollars. That activity was not only good for the city of New Orleans
but for the whole state of Louisiana as well. That being the case,
the city had to be extremely careful in terms of how it was per-
ceived throughout the rest of the world. Segregation produces
negative images which are interpreted as a city in political turmoil. This could potentiality result in the loss of millions of tourist and their dollars to the city and state. Therefore, the question
became how the city could maintain its segregationist policies
covertly while, at the same time, demonstrating peace and harmony among its citizens. I believe a pact was concluded between the city authorities and the so-called Civil Rights leaders
of the time in order to keep the peace. For example, being able

[27]

to sit anywhere on city buses in certain neighborhoods during Mardi Gras. Also, the city's mainstream media did its part.

During the carnival season, positive portrayals of people Black and White can be seen on TV having a good time. On some occasions, it will show black and white people dancing in the street together in the different neighborhoods. This positive image of New Orleans was projected all over the world. However, at the conclusion of Carnival season, the normalcy of segregation returned, only it seemed to be a little different. Jim Crow laws were slowly being phased out because of the deal that I believe was struck between city authorities and the so-called Black leaders to keep Black people in check and not have those mega demonstrations and violence which were the scourge of other Southern cities. Nevertheless, it was still dangerous to be a Black person in the cities of the Deep South.

It was inherently dangerous to be a Black person in the cities of the Deep South. I, being of young age and limited understanding, did not realize or internalize all of the danger. As small children, we knew there was a separation between the races and this separation was not only enforced by law, it was enforced by our parents. They knew the consequences which could be inflicted upon us if we were to violate those Jim Crow laws. The murder of Emmett Till in Mississippi and the lynching and murders in other Southern cities were still fresh in the minds of our parents. Therefore, our parents taught us to deal with hostile Whites and police officers.

Spring time in New Orleans is an ideal kite flying season. This is due to the fact that a constant breeze blows inland off the Mississippi River directly into my neighborhood, resulting in the sky being awash with kites transforming the neighborhood kids into flight-test engineers and designers. After school, we would gather in someone's backyard to discuss many subjects, especially how our kites were to be constructed.

Someone once said necessity is the mother of invention, however, in our case, it was a way of life. Most kites sold at the comer grocery store were upside down triangular kites without style or personality. They offered no flight challenges such as control flying and acrobatics, they just went up and came down. Also, the grocer wanted too much money for paper and two sticks. We knew we could do better than that and for a cheaper price, free!

Back in the day, all of my friends were experts in kite

construction, and like everything else, all our construction material was everywhere and in plain sight. The spokes of our kite required wood, and there was discarded lumber all over the place. The string needed for holding the spokes in place and for flying control could be found in the kitchen drawers. The paper needed for covering the kites could be found in shoe boxes and old newspapers. Finally, the kite tail was made from old rags. Looking back, my childhood world was filled with such beauty and promise; I sometimes wonder where it all went.

I have always believed that a minute amount of knowledge has more advantages than a universal amount of ignorance. This concept was demonstrated by the kids in my neighborhood on a daily basis. On one particular day during the middle of the week, we were sitting around the plum tree in my backyard eating plums and sugarcane that my father had given us when Jason, another one of our White friends, suggested we begin building our kites and on Saturday meet on the levee to fly them. We did not know it at the time, but our kites, skate-mobiles, and the other projects we constructed were all components that would prepare us for our future high school and college experience.

As we began to construct our kites, there are absolute

rules which must be followed. First, the kite must be light-weight. If the kite is too heavy, it will take too much wind in order to make it go airborne and keep it airborne. Next, the kite must be balanced in order for it to fly properly, if at all. It must be symmetrical and, finally, the bridle, the strings attached to the kite, as well as the control strings must be held by the individual flying the kite. If the bridle strings are unequal, the kite will be uncontrollable, flying to the right or left or in a continuous circle right left and crashed to the ground, which would be bad form.

When we constructed our kites, we had no idea we were employing mathematics, physics, and geometry. However, it was in our later years when we realized just how important our fun was. As previously stated, kites sold in the grocery stores were bland, featureless and cost too much. By contrast, our kites were works of art. At school, our teachers would supply us with old colorful tissue thin paper which was perfect for our kites.

Most of the kites we constructed were known as fighters. Like jet fighters, our kites were designed to destroy other kites in the sky causing them to crash into the earth. In order to build our kites as fighters, we attached what could be considered a battering ram on top of the kite. At the very tip of the battering ram, we attached a razor blade. Its primary function was to cut the string of the opposing kites or just rip up the other kites. To accomplish that task one had to be very skilled, and Jason was the very best at kite fighting. It took us several days to construct our kites and once finished we would pass them around for comments and criticism in order to make adjustments.

Saturday morning could not come quick enough for us, and once it arrived, we were ready for battle. We gathered up our kites and agreed to meet up at a specific time usually around ten in the morning at the levee. Our group consisted of Jason, Elmon, Alfred, Tommy, Lloyd and I. Before we set foot on the levees we had to cross approximately four sets of railroad tracks. This was another benefit we kids took advantage of. This was the era of the locomotive engine and just watching them speed down the track was inspiring. To children, especially black children, the locomotive, and the levees were unintended gifts allowed by the city. There was no segregation or signs which read "Colored Only "or "White Only "on those tracks or levees. As we crossed the tracks and walked up to the summit of the levee, there were large ships going to and from. Due to the fact that New Orleans is so flat and the Mississippi River Levees are so high, we had a panoramic view of a large portion of the city.

As we looked around the levee, there were kids flying kites everywhere. The sky was awash with kites, so much so we had to walk a short distance in order to have some kite flying space. As we held up our kites above our heads, the wind took hold, and they immediately took to the sky. Jason's kite begins to fly wildly. However, he remained in control of its flight path. He guided his kite toward mine, and I guided my kite towards his. We flew our kites like jet fighters, making passes and trying to cut the string or just damage the opposing kite. At this point, Jason flew his kite in such a way it began to gain altitude and then took a nose dive directly for my kite. They crashed into each other and became tangled, crashing to earth. A cheer went up as we raced to our kites. As we disentangled them, we could see that there was minor damage which we repaired on site and launched them into the sky once again. Our kites did exactly what they were designed to do.

Standing on the levee and looking around at all the kids

playing and having a good time without any segregationist policies separating us, I have often wondered throughout my adult life why Jim Crow laws were necessary. Separating us was more harmful to the development of children than uniting us. I think Black parents were more aware of that situation than White parents and that is why Jim Crow did not exist in my backyard. At the end of our day on the levee, we walked back to the neighborhood discussing the events of the day.

As we sat around talking about how our kites went on the attack, I noticed my kite had some damage to it. When we were flying our kites, I noticed Jason's kite came very close to my mine, however, I didn't think there had been any contact. Once all my friends saw my damaged kite, they began to inspect theirs. My kite was the only one damaged. Then the fun began, and they all started on me saying I had no idea of how to fly a fighting kite. The more they ragged on me, the angrier I became, and I did not try to hide my anger. But, the difference between today's angry kids and the angry kids of yesterday was the absence of violence. This is not to say we didn't fight between us because we did and I had my share. What we did not have was the extreme violence associated with our fights. When it was all said, and done, at the end of our arguments and fights we remained good friends' and, most importantly, we stayed alive.

My father, Mr. Joe, as he was known throughout the community was, in my opinion, one of the few Black men that White parents trusted with their children. I imagine this was due to the fact that he had two issues he and they could identify with, his business required him to be in their homes on a daily basis, whereby they knew him very well, and he looked like them. In other words, he was able to go back and forth across the color line. However, this was not unusual within the city of New Orleans. In my neighborhood, there were a number of people who could pass for White. We kids waited excitedly for my father to arrive home during the day because we knew we would be taking a ride in the truck to the icehouse.

Approximately one to two miles from my house was the ice-house where all of the ice-men and others in the area went to purchase ice. Once Mr. Joe came home, and after eating lunch, he would gather my friends, tell them to inform their parents they were going to the ice-house with him. Once this was accomplished, we climbed into the truck and off we went to the ice-house. When we arrived, my father would back the truck up to the dock where we jumped off the truck onto the dock and waited for him. As we walked into the building, the first thing we noticed was how cold it was, and there were these huge blocks of ice stacked in orderly rows. After he had placed his order, we went back to the dock and watched as the ice was being loaded on the truck. When this task was finished, we jumped back onto the truck and away we went. When we arrived home, my father gave me a bag of crushed ice to give my mother for lemonade and back to work he went. My mother gave each of us a cup of lemonade, and we proceeded to climb on the roof to talk about what we were going to do next.

From time to time, my father would allow me to accompany him as he made his rounds selling ice. He began his day between four and five am. I would be so excited to know I would be going with him I'd be up dressed and waiting on him. We traveled all over the neighborhood and visited many different households. Yet, they all seemed to have one thing in common, they all seemed to be very glad to see my Honey, and they all seemed to know me. All of the ladies of the houses would come over to me and kiss me regardless of their race. This is how I became friends with my white buddies.

There was a function in my neighborhood which everybody looked forward to, especially the kids, and that function

was known as a "Supper". During the summer, suppers were
held every weekend. Sometimes at the homes of more than one
family depending on the area. The menus were different and
very delicious. There were chicken dinners of all types with all
the trimmings, BBQ dinners, fish dinners, vegetables of all
types and many other items. Also, the price was right about
two dollars a plate. The function of the suppers was to raise extra money for families. Everybody in the neighborhood supported the family who was having a supper, even the white
families. They would send their kids to place their orders. I did
not know if the White families had suppers, but if they did the
Black families would have supported them. If there were more
than one family in the area having a supper, the families having
the suppers would place orders with each other in order to
show support.

    The suppers were another way we were able to interact
with each other. It didn't matter what family was engaged in
having a supper; all the neighborhood kids would come together and wait for free food. Towards the end of the supper,
all of the leftover food which could not be stored was given
away, and the number one item on our menu was fried chicken.
Also, we delivered dinners to seniors and the shut-ins usually

the suppers were an all-day affair.

My neighborhood, for all practical purposes, was a very peaceful place to live and grow up. Crime, for the most part, was nonexistent and we rarely observed the police patrolling the area. We did not have an official neighborhood watch program, but due to the fact that the vast majority of the residents were either family members or knew each other very well, very little went on without it soon becoming public knowledge. This included Black and White families. Plus, there were people walking around the neighborhood at all hours of the day and night. We rarely paid very much attention to Jim Crow laws as long as we remained within the neighborhood. However, venturing outside was another story.

The few times we did venture out was usually to travel to the one and only colored amusement park in the city, Lincoln Beach. Whites had a number of amusement parks they could visit, but the primary amusement park that most of them visited were Pontchartrain Beach and the difference between the two parks was striking. The justifications the South used to justify segregation, and the separation of the races was with the creation of the "Separate but Equal" policy. To see just how unequal, the separate but equal the policy was, one only needed to observe the differences between the two beaches.

I've never been on the inside of Pontchartrain Beach because I was prohibited from doing so, but when my family and I would travel along Lake Shore Drive, we would have an unobstructed view of the park. It was huge with a gigantic roller coaster located at the entrance of the park. Plus, the park was built on the lovely beach of Lake Pontchartrain which extended for miles. By contrast, Lincoln beach was small and compact. Its portion of the beach of Lake Pontchartrain extended approximately one hundred yards, and its main feature was the swimming pool which was always crowded due to the fact that at that time period, it was the only place in the city which had a pool open to blacks. Also, from my neighborhood, Lincoln Beach was located on the opposite end of the city which made it a difficult travel destination.

When we utilized the city buses to travel to Lincoln Beach or any other place which required us to venture outside the neighborhood, the segregation laws were strictly enforced. I can recall standing in the back of the bus which was extremely crowded with my mother looking at all those empty seats reserved for whites in the front of the bus. For us, the main reason for visiting the park was the swimming pool.

However due to the distance, we had to travel, and the stupidity of what we had to put up with, plus the fact that we had something not too many people in the city had, which was a backyard swimming pool, our visits to the park were rare.

In my neighborhood baseball was the game of choice. We did not have a park to play ball in the neighborhood, so we had to improvise. The street which runs along the side of my house was our baseball diamond. It was wide enough and obviously long enough. Our bat was a sawed-off broom handle, first base was a parked car on the right, second base was a pot hole, third base was a parked car on the left and home-plate was a garbage can lid. Our baseball was an old rubber ball which was hard enough to hit and soft enough to catch bare-handed. We would play baseball-stick-ball for hours on end, and I do believe some of my childhood friends could have gone pro by the way they played as children.

As I have stated previously, there was a levee which divided Orleans Parish from Jefferson Parish and this levee was the meeting place for the kids in the neighborhood. We became very good friends just by hanging out there. One of the incidents which caused us to hang out there was the lottery. In the evening after school, all of the kids would head for Jefferson

Jim Crow Did Not Exist in my Backyard

Parish via the levee to play the lottery. Although it was an illegal lottery, it did not stop the good citizens of New Orleans from indulging with the hope of hitting it big, and when I say hitting it big it meant winning forty or fifty dollars. That was big money in those days. Everybody knew where the lottery agents were located, including the police, and we were never harassed. I can recall from time to time seeing police cars parked near the lottery place. Also, I can recall to this day playing my mother's favorite numbers, 3 13 33 and 4 11 44 among others. After playing the numbers, we would gather on the levee to have a good time. We would get to know new friends and renew old friendships. Also, observing White and Black kids walking home together was a normal thing in the neighborhood, unusual considering what was going on at the time.

Mr. James Brown wrote a song, "Say It Loud I'm Black and I'm Proud". Well, during my childhood we were neither Black nor proud of being Black. As a matter-of-fact to be called Black was considered fighting words when we were in school. The vast majority of books we studied from were written by Whites whose views of African Americans were a little right of being human. The dictionaries of the time were no exception. According to the dictionaries, the term black is defined as "wicked, very sad or gloomy, unfriendly, spoiled, unclean; a person who could not be trusted and dangerous". As kids, we were taught that the dictionaries spoke the truth and it was your reference book to find the meaning of words.

We the little "colored" kids were powerless and ignorant as to the way we were taught regarding of our identity. Therefore, the way the dictionary defined Black was not the way we looked upon ourselves, resulting in the fact that being called black was taboo among us. Plus, our White friends did not look upon us in that fashion.

On the other hand, Whites had no problem with being called White and their children proudly proclaimed that they were, in fact, White. This attitude was reinforced by those same dictionaries defining white as "not intended to cause harm, free from spot or blemish, pure, innocent, the opposite of black.

Children were extremely truthful unless they were forced to act or speak falsely by others who have power over them. When my friends and I got together, we would talk and act out everything as it related to a kids' world. Not once to the best of my recollection were there any incidents of derogatory name calling directed at anybody within my circle of friends. I truly believe that because of my father's association with other families in the neighborhood racial harmony was enjoyed by all. It can, therefore, be said that Jim Crow laws seem to have worked with most White adults during that period. However, it had an unintended consequence I am sure the city authorities never realized. In spite of the segregated schools, theaters, parks, and everyplace else, the kids in my neighborhood continued to get along.

A perfect example of the phenomenon was the illegal lottery or as pronounced in New Orleans, "lottery". My home was located in Orleans Parish in the Carrollton section of the city. About three blocks to the west of where I lived was the Jefferson Parish line. Separating the two parishes was a levee running approximately north and south for about three miles. As far as I knew, both White and Black families played the lottery. The prize money was not big, maybe twenty or thirty dollars, but back in the fifties and sixties that amount of money went a long way.

Although the lottery was illegal at that time, the authorities never bothered anybody who played it. The Parish Sheriff knew exactly where the numbers hall was located. Sometimes we would see their cars parked in the vicinity and they would just sit there. Sometimes the sheriff would call us over to his car, give us some money and a slip of paper. When we returned, they would give us a nickel or dime. Unlike today, we never feared the police. As a matter of fact, we rarely saw them in the neighborhood due to the fact that there was no crime there. Outside the neighborhood is where the police harassment occurred. Our neighborhood was extremely stable. There were no gangs, no guns in the hands of children, no drugs and parental and community control of its children was absolute.

During my childhood, there was a saying which stated "spare the rod, spoil the child". In my case and that of my friends, sparing the rod was never an option when we disobeyed our parents or other parents in the neighborhood. This activity did not cause us any behavioral problems in the future that I am aware of. In today's world, I do not condone corporal punishment of children. Studies have proven that it does produce negative behavioral activities. Besides, it was a different world, a different time and situation.

One day we were sitting in the backyard eating t-cakes when someone began telling the story of the last time he, as we would say, caught a whipping. We all could relate to his story as we all found ourselves at the business end of a switch or belt from time to time, but Tommy's story was the most interesting. He relays the story of a time when he disobeyed his mother, resulting in a whipping administered by her. In his backyard, there was an old peach tree. It didn't bear much fruit but what it did bear was sweet and juicy.

Although our community was segregated, our manners were not. Being disrespectful was not tolerated. Tommy's mother's name was Helene Wagner. To all the kids she was known as Miss Helene. All of the parents in the community were referred to as Miss or Mr. and their first name, whether they were Black or White.

Miss Helene told Tommy to pick a switch from that old peach tree in the backyard. This was the preferred instrument used by Southern mothers to chastise their children. A switch is a slender, very pliable tree limb with no leaves on it. It never breaks, even under the most extreme conditions. I know I can attest to its durability. When Tommy approached the peach tree, he said he spotted the perfect switch. It was about six inches long with some leaves remaining on it. He removed the tiny switch and presented it to his mother thinking she would find it funny, start laughing and forget about whipping him.

[45]

Well, needless to say, it didn't work because she became even angrier. He said she stormed out of the kitchen into the backyard and retrieved her own switch. When she came back into the kitchen, it looked like she was carrying the entire tree, according to Tommy. He said he knew he was in for it. He had to come up with a plan, and quick.

We sat there listening to him, knowing we had all been through the same ordeal at some point, and laughing at him at the same time. Tommy's mother was not a small woman. She was short, plump, and she smoked. After thinking about it for a short while, he came up with a plan. He had used it a few times before with mixed results. However, there was a problem, his sisters. He had two sisters, one younger and another older. He and his older sister did not get along at all. Anything he did which his sister thought their mother should know about, she would tell on him. Don't get me wrong Miss Helene did not show favoritism towards any of her children. However, she knew Tommy was a hyperactive kid who required extra discipline. His relationship with his younger sister, Mary, was much closer, as long as he kept her from being influenced by his older sister, Angela. When Tommy's mother came back inside carrying that tree-trunk of a switch, Angela began singing,

Jim Crow Did Not Exist in my Backyard

you're going to get it, you're going to get it. At this time, according to Tommy, his mother called to him. When he approached her, she took a swing at him and he jumped back causing the switch to miss his legs. When she moved towards him, Tommy took off with his mother giving chase. Angela attempted to catch and hold him, but he brushed her off. As Miss Helene was chasing Tommy her being overweight and a smoker caught up with her. She began to cough uncontrollably. Tommy had seen this situation with his mother before, but not this bad. She had to stop and sit on the edge of her bed, with the switch falling from her hand to the floor.

Tommy and his sisters became very concerned as they rushed over to their mother to comfort her. Tommy and his mother were very close, with him being her only son and all. He began to hug and kiss her as he kicked the switch under the bed. For the remainder of the evening, they gave great care and love to their mother. The next day, everything was back to normal. That was the last time Tommy gave his mother cause to retrieve a switch.

A few years later, Miss Helene joined my Honey in heaven. Tommy's story was not unique in our community; we all lived it.

As I think about the way we lived as children and compare and contrast the way kids live today, I don't know how they would have survived in those days, in the same manner as we did. As I have stated previously, I lived in an era of severe racial separation. I will not expound on it; suffice it to say that it is a well-known historical fact. Jim Crow policies controlled all aspects of Southern life in New Orleans, publicly and privately, however not so much when social contact was under the radar. As I have once stated, for every action there is an equal and opposite reaction. African Americans' rights were denied under Jim Crow. White Americans' rights were enhanced under those same laws. Or were they?

The right of association gives all Americans the right to be in the company of those whom they choose, not the government. However, this was not true back in the time of Jim Crow. Blacks could not associate with whites socially, or in most cases, professionally unless the interest of Whites was at hand. In contrast, Whites could associate with anyone they chose to, or so they thought. In some cases, Whites could be arrested for socializing with blacks without a good reason. This is where the neighborhood kids came in. Therefore, it could be said that

Jim Crow Did Not Exist in my Backyard

Jim Crow restricted Whites as well as Blacks. In today's world, I don't think Whites would tolerate that situation, not being able to associate with Blacks or anyone as a matter of law.

Most of our White friends did not visit the area public pools. They knew we, their Black friends, were not allowed. We did what was necessary. The limitations placed on us required us to do things differently. It rained often, and in most cases severely, in New Orleans. Yet, rain storms were a constant friend to us, kids, especially during the summer.

Heavy rain and flooding in New Orleans were major problems for those who had to manage the situation. However, to the children in my neighborhood, it was a godsend. The flood waters became our lakes, creeks, and streams to enjoy. The heavy rain became our showers to play in.

As soon as we noticed that a rain storm was imminent, we would run into our homes, change into our swimsuits and head back outside. From what I can recall, we had so much fun. We rode our bicycles in the storm, went skating and played all sorts of games in the rain. Sometimes when we noticed a flooded area, it instantly became our swimming pool. In some instances, the flooding was deep enough we were able to swim under water. I can say that not one of us ever got hurt or became sick from doing this. Furthermore, playing in the rain was a constant activity. I cannot imagine today's parents allowing their kids to *be kids* in this way.

The National Football League has instituted a program for kids called Play60. It's a program which allows children to go outside and play for sixty minutes each day. If this program had been in effect when I was a child, the kids in my community and throughout the country would have thought we were being punished. For kids, back then playing outside was not an option but a necessity. As a matter-of-fact, our parents pushed us outside to play in order to keep us out of their hair all day. This was the era of flying kites, not flying on the Internet. We built our skateboards. Toys-R-Us was never an option because there was no such place in order to purchase them at that time. Playing football or stickball outside rather than playing those same games in our bedrooms on some computer screen. After lunch and dinner, we would go outside to climb trees, fly our kites and pick and eat fresh nothing compared to this major problem facing children today. The answers to those problems are in plain sight.

The climate in New Orleans is an enigma for those non-residents of the city, especially during the winter. Unlike the summer when it is hot, humid, and rainy most of the time, winter was most enjoyable. Don't get me wrong, we kids loved the summer, if for no other reason than the fact that school was closed. Thank God my father was an iceman. Winter, on the other hand, is short and not very cold. One day it would be so cold we would have to make our way over ice puddles left from the previous day's rain. The next day we would be outside in short sleeves and shorts riding our bicycles.

On this one particular day, I was in my backyard chewing on sugarcane my father had planted in his garden. It was an unusually warm day in February when I heard a voice calling me. I looked up and saw that it was Jason and Elmon sitting on top of a little shed, our usual meeting place. We engaged in small talk for a while until someone said let's go fishing. When I nodded to say yes, Jason jumped off the roof saying he was going to get Tommy. Elmon also jumped off the roof and ran to his house to retrieve his fishing pole.

Our fishing poles were not technologically advanced, but they worked. They consisted of a cane pole with an old fishing line and hooks we found lying around the house. We used small bolts to act as sinkers. When my friends returned, we set off in search of bait. After getting a shovel from the shed, we began looking for a good area to dig for earthworms. Fortunately, it had rained the day before making it easy to dig into the soil. The first shovel full of soil produced more nice fat juicy worms then we could count. After notifying our parents of what we were going to do and where we were going, we were on our way.

We fished in the Mississippi River in a small sandy area on the opposite side of the levee. When we arrived, there were two other kids fishing. We all set our lines out on the bottom because that's where the catfish were.

Catfish was our favorite fish to catch because they were the easiest to reel in and they were delicious. Most mothers could cook catfish so well; it made your mouth water just thinking about it. Because New Orleans was predominately Catholic, frying fish could be smelled throughout the neighborhood, especially on Fridays.

After sitting around and waiting for a few minutes, I noticed a slight tug on my line and so did Jason on his. We jumped up, secured our polls, gave them a tug and begin pulling in our lines. When I pulled my line in there was a catfish on the other end. It was about twelve inches long and weighed about a pound and a half. The same was true for Jason. At the end of our fishing trip, everybody had caught fish. This is why we liked fishing so much. Very rarely was there a time when we didn't catch anything. The Mississippi River is blessed with an abundant amount of fish, catfish being one of them. On our way home we made two new friends as we laughed, joked, and compared our fish. God, did I love my childhood. Why did it have to end?

According to Jim Crow Laws and the segregationist laws of New Orleans, our fishing trips and all the other activities we engaged in were illegal. Why? Our activities were considered integrated and strictly forbidden. If the State had wanted to push the issue, Black kids could have been jailed or worse. It had occurred in the South. However, we did not worry about such things. Politics was not a very important subject to children, regardless of race. Only later in life did it become a factor.

When I returned home after our fishing trip, I presented my mother with the fish I had caught. I saw how pleased she was as she placed the fish in the kitchen sink. I stood next to her and watched her as she began to clean the fish. It was Friday and a school holiday.

For Catholics, Friday was known as meatless Friday, which meant no Catholic, under the consequence of sin, could eat meat on Friday. The exception to that rule was poultry and fish. Many non-Catholic families observe this tradition, not because it was a sin but because it seemed to be the right thing to do. Sometimes we would eat dinner on Fridays with our Catholic neighbors. Throughout the neighborhood, the smell of fish being fried permeated every nostril. In the evening all seemed right with the world.

When I speak of my backyard, I am not only speaking of my immediate backyard behind my house. I also include my neighbor's backyard, my neighborhood, and to some extent, the levees of the Mississippi River and the New Orleans Transportation Authority. All transportation, public and private, was segregated including taxis, ambulances, school buses and even the family car, especially in the case of a black man and a white woman in a car together. If she was not sitting in the back seat of the car, there was a ninety-nine percent chance they would be stopped by the police if spotted.

With all of those obstacles placed before us we were still able to go beyond those racist laws just to interact with our friends. Of all the modes of public transportation in the city, the streetcar became our personal play toy. The streetcar was an electric vehicle which ran on railroad tracks with a railroad train undercarriage. Unlike the trolleys of San Francisco, which were powered by an electrical underground chain, sprocket, and pulley system, New Orleans streetcars were powered by an overhead electrical cable. There was a long pole extending from the cable to the streetcar, supplying it with the power necessary to run its engines, resulting in movement along the tracks. Unlike the buses which had one driver, the streetcar had two conductors. This was due to the fact that passengers were able to board and exit at each end.

There was a huge difference when riding the buses as opposed to riding the streetcars. The white bus drivers seemed to be more racist when dealing with black adults and children. However, when the bus was proceeding along its route in an all-black neighborhood, some bus drivers allowed us to sit anywhere we wanted, as long as there were no whites on board. Just before a white person boarded the bus, we were told to move to our segregated seating are. Also, while waiting for the bus along with other passengers, white and black, we were not allowed to get on the bus before the whites. With all of those obstacles placed before us, we still knew how to circumvent some of those segregationist laws, and we used the streetcar to do it.

If I didn't know any better, I would say that the street-car was designed for kids and fun. First, they were roomy with moveable seats. They looked like a giant toy, and the conductors were much more reasonable when interacting with us. I imagine this was due to the fact that there were two of them on the streetcar and they did not have to pay much attention to the road since the streetcar rode on rails.

Between the hours of seven and eight in the morning and three and four thirty in the afternoon Monday through Friday, the streetcar would be loaded with kids including myself. That situation was a result of there being two Catholic schools on the streetcar route, one white and the other black. Although we went to separate schools, some of us lived in the same neighborhood, and we knew each other. Therefore, our white friends introduced us to their friends, and we introduced them to our friends. Over time we all became friends, even with the little white girls. With the exception of the neighborhood kids, the only other place we were able to interact was on the streetcar.

Most of the conductors on the streetcars were pleasant and non-confrontational. I would assume that this was due to the fact that there were two of them on duty on the streetcar.

Jim Crow Did Not Exist in my Backyard

While one was driving the other was interacting with us. Another factor which allowed the conductors to interact with us was the streetcar, for the most part, did not run on the street; it ran on what is known in New Orleans as the neutral ground. This was a grassy area with two sets of tracks for outbound and inbound streetcars. It was in the center with two two-lane streets for inbound and outbound car traffic. The only area where the conductors had to pay close attention where the cross streets which ran across the tracks in the opposite direction. However, only one of the conductors accomplished this task at a time. This allowed the conductors to interact with us on a personal level.

When riding public transportation, the difference in behavior directed toward black passengers by the bus drivers as oppose to their counterparts on the streetcars was quite noticeable. Generally speaking, bus drivers strictly enforced the segregationist policies of the city. They rarely interacted with us and when they did it was usually in a hostile and threatening manor. On the other hand, the streetcar conductors made life a little easier and a lot more fun while we lived under such harsh laws. During the time we rode the streetcars in droves during school hours, we were allowed to sit with our friends on any seat we wanted, if only for a short time. We knew where the racial lines were drawn and rarely did we cross them. When we did, and when there were white adults on board, we were told, in a non-threatening manner, to behave. After school hours, strict adherence to the segregationist laws was enforced, which was all right with us because of the fact that we rarely rode public transportation in the evening anyway. In a way, the streetcar became part of my extended backyard because it allowed us to interact with our friends as much as we did in my backyard.

During my childhood as well as that of my friends, notwithstanding our educational experiences, adventure, playing, and just having fun during our free time were key elements to the way our lives were to be structured in the future. Other than the death of my father, I can't recall any other incident that had a profound impact on me and the other kids in the neighborhood, except one. With the death of my father, we knew that there would be no more ice chips and climbing onto the ice truck in order to enter our air-conditioned hideout on those unbearable hot summer days. No more money under my house for us kids to gather knowing full well that my father put it there. But most of all there would never be another swimming pool in my backyard for the neighborhood kids to enjoy during our long hot summer. Then, one morning it happened. It wasn't a swimming pool, but something just as good. Summer changed over to winter.

Early one winter morning I was lying in my bed. Not sleeping, just lying there. Suddenly I heard this voice outside my window. The person was running around the neighborhood yelling, "It's snowing, it's snowing!" I jumped out of my bed to see what all the commotion was about. When I looked out my window, I could not believe my eyes. It was indeed snowing. Big, white snowflakes which appeared to be cotton balls were falling from the sky. I had never seen such a thing. By this time everyone in my household was up, and I would assume the same for the other households in the neighborhood. People began to come out of their homes onto the streets with arms extended and dancing.

Finally, after overcoming my state of shock, I rushed to get dressed in order to join those people already outside. When I walked outside onto my back porch, I felt the first snowflake fall onto my face. It was a cold, strange feeling and as soon as it landed it was gone. The snow began to accumulate on the grassy area in my backyard and on the rooftops. I leaped from the porch onto the snowy grass and rolled around as if I were a madman. My dog Blackie joined me. He had never seen snow either. Then I heard the excited voices of others yelling, "It's snowing," including my friends. I ran out of my backyard onto the street and joined my friends to share in their fun.

Cold winter weather and New Orleans appear to be contradictory on the surface. To me, as best as I can explain it, New Orleans had two seasons, summer and winter. During the summer it was hot, rainy and humid with mosquitoes all the time. During the winter, on the other hand, we experienced all four seasons. I can recall during the winter season having to bundle up with hats, scarves, and coats because it was that cold. Yet, I can also recall playing outside in short sleeves and shorts or playing in a rain shower because it was that hot. Presently, it is the week of February 17, 2013. Where I live in Tobyhanna, Pennsylvania, the temperature is twenty degrees and snowing. However, in New Orleans, for this same week, the temperature is projected to be between sixty-five and eighty degrees. I would love to be there right now.

On this day, of course, school was closed along with just about everything else. There were no vehicles on the roads, and therefore, my neighborhood became a winter wonder and play land. But, we had a problem. What were we going to do with this snow now that we had it? We had no sleds or toboggans or any other winter toys to play with. What we did have however were our brains, and we knew how to use them.

It can be said that necessity is the true mother of invention. Unlike today's kids who rely on X-Box and PlayStation consoles, we relied on our tools, supplies, mathematics, and the deductive reasoning our brains supplied. We had to think outside the box in order to solve some of our complex problems, for example using geometry when constructing our skate mobiles or when using Newton's law, "For *every action, there is an equal and opposite reaction".* We were deciding on the type of shoes we would wear to thrust our skate mobile down the road as fast as it could go. In my world as a child, television did not play an important part in my life as it does in the lives of today's kids. This allowed us to interact with our environment to solve problems which would otherwise go unsolved. Sadly, the impact of non-involvement in the environment of today's kids is reflected in the world's ranking as it relates to Science and Mathematics. School-aged children in the United States are ranked twenty-fifth when compared to other school-aged children in other countries. This would be unheard of back then.

The snow kept falling and falling as we began to think of ways we could maximize our fun provided by this gift from the heavens. We began consulting with each other on how we could do this. Lloyd came up with the idea of using cardboard boxes as our sleds. It worked on the grassy levees during the summer, and surely it could work on snow. Next, I thought of tire inner-tubes. Car tires came with inner-tubes. Tubeless tires were not as common as they are today and there were many inner tubes lying around everybody's backyard.

The inner-tubes would be perfect. We used them as flotation devices on the water when we went to the beach. If they worked on water and grass, certainly they could work on snow. We went about gathering some inner-tubes only to find them flat. It must be remembered, every kid in my neighborhood had bicycles and on those bicycles were tires and within those tires were inner-tubes, which went flat from time to time. When that happened, we did not have the money to have them repaired. So, we had to come up with an alternative. There were at least one or two kids whose fathers had inter-tube tire repair kits and a hand air pump. My father had those items on hand and, from time to time, we would use them to repair the tires on our bikes. Every one of us knew how to dismantle our bikes, remove the tire, inner tube repair it and put it back together. The knowledge to accomplish that task was a must if we wanted to ride our bikes.

We assembled the inner-tubes in my father's garage, hooked them up to the air pump hoping there were no holes in them. We began pumping them up, and to our surprise, they held the air. We gathered them and headed for the levee, those levees closest to our house. When we arrived, there were kids from everywhere it seemed. They were using their inner-tubes and boxes sliding down the levee. We joined in and all had a great time.

As we were having our fun, we did not notice the snow falling had begun to slack up, and there were some blue patches in the sky which could be observed. But we didn't care. There was more than enough snow on the ground to do what we wanted to do. Then the snow stopped, and after a while, we decided it was time to go home. By this time the snow was covering everything even the street. We placed our inter-tubes in the garage and departed for our individual homes wondering if the snow will still be there tomorrow. The sunset in the evening was spectacular; I had never seen anything like it before. On that day, for us, Jim Crow did not exist.

As children, almost everything we were engaged in benefited us educationally and helped us with the lessons we had to learn later on in life. One of those tools was playing marbles. Before I knew how marbles would be advantageous for my future, let me discuss the marble games we played. The first game was called bull ring. A giant circle was drawn in the dirt and in the middle of that circle, a smaller circle. Within that smaller circle, a previously established number of marbles were placed. There was one small marble called the beanie which was placed in the center of the normal-sized marbles. Usually, up to five players could play. The object of the game was to knock out as many marbles as you could from the large circle while shooting your marble from outside the line of the large circle. Also, if a shooter knocked out the beanie from the large circle, the shooter would win all the remaining marbles. At the end of the game, the shooter with the most marbles won and he would shoot first for the next game.

The next game we played was called fish. This is a game where one of us would draw a symbol of what resembled a fish minus the tail in the dirt. Once again, we would meet to decide how many marbles each of us would place in the fish.

Jim Crow Did Not Exist in my Backyard

At this point, we would walk about ten to fifteen feet from the fish and draw a line behind which all the shooters had to stand or kneel behind prior to shooting. If a shooter shot his marble in front of that line, it was considered a foul and he would lose his turn to shoot.

The object of the game was to shoot as many marbles out of the fish without the shooter's marble stopping in the fish. If that happened, the shooter would have to replace the marble he knocked out of the fish, if any, and lose his turn to shoot. This game was much easier to play, and we preferred it to bull ring which had too many rules and was more difficult.

The two best shooters in the entire neighborhood were Leslie and Jason. I believe these two guys stayed up nights practicing their shooting skills. This is reflected in the number of marbles they own.

I called my generation the hands-on generation because almost everything we did required the use of our brains which was reflected in our hands. Our skate mobiles, kites, flotation devices, toboggans, marble games along with others contributed to our educational experiences we would need later on in life. Our construction of our skate mobiles taught us how to construct geometric figures and angles. Our kite flying taught us how to solve the problems associated with aerodynamics. The construction of our flotation devices taught us about positive and negative pressure and what causes some materials to sink and others to float. Our cardboard toboggans were magnificent in their simplicity. We learned that speed, or the amount of it, was directly related to the amount of friction encountered in the environment. So, when riding our toboggans, we looked for the steepest decline and shortest grassy areas on the levee. We did not realize it at the time, but we were teaching ourselves physics. However, in my opinion, our most important lesson we learned were associated with our marble playing. Our marble playing taught us how to add, subtract, multiply and divide. Using marbles, we learned how to buy and sell, barter and trade. Back then, as far as a kid was concerned, marbles and not money determined wealth. Therefore, at an early age, we learned it was far better to be wealthy than poor.

As I look back and think about my backyard and the problems associated with it, I realize that Jim Crow laws possessed the seeds for its own destruction. The basic problem with them was that they were too definitive, meaning, the color of one's skin trumped everything else. For example, if I were an African American millionaire during the time of Jim Crow and I had enough money to buy anything I wanted, considering the fact that my money was as green as everybody else's, I would not have been able to buy a first-class train ticket or sit anywhere I wanted to while traveling in the South.

There were no discretionary judgment calls when dealing with a person-to-person situation. Case in point Mrs. Rosa Parks. In 1955, Mrs. Parks was jailed for not giving up her seat to a white man while riding public transportation in Montgomery Alabama. The bus driver could have told the white man that she had just gotten off from work, she was tired and to try and find another seat. Of course, this did not happen. If it had, along with Mrs. Parks, the bus driver would have gone to jail.

Another problem associated with Jim Crow laws was monetary. In all public and private buildings, such as government, schools, movie theaters, restaurants, lunch counters, and hospitals there had to be two of everything, one white and the other colored. Money and Jim Crow were strange bedfellows, and in the early days of Jim Crow, money was of little importance as long as the Coloreds remained in their place. However, the fact still remained if there were two of everything, funds had to be allocated for both. Logic would dictate that this policy was totally irrational, yet the policy remained in effect until it began to come apart almost a hundred years later. During that period of time, the Colored citizens of the United States of America, the land of the free and the home of the brave, suffered in much of the same way the Jews did under the Pharaohs of Egypt and the Black South Africans under apartheid. For generations, black people suffered under those laws. Even two world wars could not achieve any meaningful change. Millions of people resigned themselves to the fact that Jim crow would always be the law of the land in the South. Yet on December 1, 1955, one brave Black woman with the simple utterance of the word "NO" changed the course of history for this country and the world for all time.

Strangely as all of this was taking place the sting of racism and discrimination did not impact me or my friends in the same manner as it did the children of Tallahatchie County, Mississippi during that time period. In Mississippi, the battle lines were drawn and strictly enforced. If any Colored person strayed across the line, it could have meant a death sentence, and in most instances, that is exactly what happened.

New Orleans, on the other hand, was more cosmopolitan when dealing with its citizens. While segregation and Jim Crow Laws were deeply entrenched in the city, violations of those laws did not usually result in a death sentence. Before Hurricane Katrina, New Orleans was known as the queen city of the South, sorry Atlanta. Presently, it is still known as the Big Easy. Prior to the National Football League and the Super Bowl making their appearance in the city, New Orleans held two events which gained worldwide and national attention, The Mardi Gras and the Sugar Bowl. People from all over the country and the world traveled to New Orleans in order to participate in those two events.

The Sugar Bowl placed New Orleans prominently on the map of the United States, and the Mardi Gras placed the city prominently on the world map. At that time, the Sugar Bowl game was played at Tulane Stadium which was a part of Tulane University, a segregated, white, Protestant, male school. My neighborhood was approximately two miles from the university, yet my family and other black families in the neighborhood and the city did not take part in the festivities associated with the Sugar Bowl. This was due to the fact that it was segregated. The most prominent school in the state, LSU, frequently played in that game.

As a child, I do not recall seeing any confederate flags

flying in the city with one exception, Sugar Bowl Sunday, especially if Old Miss was playing in the game. There were Confederate flags flapping in the wind everywhere throughout the city, except in the black neighborhoods. All of the events associated with the Sugar Bowl were segregated. No black family in my neighborhood, and I am sure, other black families in their neighborhood ventured outside of them as it would have been too dangerous. One might ask how dangerous was it? Consider a black person in the downtown area of the French Quarter being surrounded by hundreds of drunken, racist, white people from Mississippi and New Orleans waving their little Confederate flags. The results would be obvious. Also, those Northern white liberals, and there were some of them at that time, who traveled to the city to attend the game did seem to enjoy a little of what Jim Crow provided. To paraphrase Dr. King, *it is not the loud voices of a minority of bad white folks shouting bigotry and hatred, but the quietness of a majority of the good white folks who did and said nothing.* In today's world, I sometimes wonder how did black players of Old Miss or any other Southern college or university that holds the Confederate Flag as a badge of honor feel having to play under that

Jim Crow Did Not Exist in my Backyard

banner, knowing what that flag represents. It has to be a dilemma for them.

Mardi Gras was a different story. Everybody took part in the celebration. Of course, the restrictions were still in place with a few exceptions. All of the hotels, restaurants, and bars in the French Quarter and throughout the city were segregated. Yet, the city authorities knew they could not piss off a large portion of the population with those harsh restrictive laws, so some were relaxed. The tourist industry played an essential role in the economic vitality of the city, pre-Katrina. This is evident when millions upon millions of people descend on the city during Mardi Gras season. This would not be the case if New Orleans were engulfed in political and racial turmoil. To this day, I believe that the so-called black leaders of the day and the city's authorities came to some type of agreement which kept the black population from exploding as it was about to happen in other major cities. Be that as it may, I can report that as kids, Mardi Gras season was the high point of having fun and a good time regardless of skin color.

In my neighborhood, on Mardi Gras day all the children masqueraded in a costume of one kind or another. I had my Hop Along Cassidy outfit; Tommy wore his Superman getup, and Elmon was in a made up monster costume. This was the accepted standard of the time, and most of the costumes represented a white superhero. Other than our fathers, the black kids did not have a strong male in the newsprint or television media we could identify with. This was one of the negative effects of Jim Crow. However, we flipped that negative effect into a positive one. I can think of no other man I would rather be other than my father. Yet that lack of a positive black male role model, in my opinion, can trace its origins all the way back to slavery.

Throughout history, and to some extent the present, slavery has existed in one form or another. In the United States, slavery had existed for hundreds of years until its final end at the conclusion of the Civil War. Yet the effects of slavery can still be felt today. Slavery and the economic vitality of the South were so interwoven it went from being a system of class or, as a white southerner would say, remembering to stay in your place, to an institution. After the slave trade and its transportation of human cargo had become illegal throughout the world, it became entrenched in the United States. Finally, in 1807 the Slave Importation Act was introduced in Congress. This act prohibited the importation of slaves. The act became law in 1808. With the introduction of this law, slavery went from being a station of existence in life or a class system to an institution or, in today's language, a corporation which dealt in commodities in the South. Although there existed a United States Navy at the time. It was small and could not effectively enforce the law; this was not true of the British Navy which was huge. They could enforce the law which, in effect, ended the transportation of slaves.

The Southern aristocratic plantation owners and slave masters realize that without the importation of African slaves their economic future was in jeopardy. The solution to this problem was in plain sight, the slave himself. As a result, slave breeding plantations came into being with their primary function being the constant production of slaves. These breeding plantations sprang up all over the South with the largest concentration of them being in the lower South. The crises brought on by the new law had been solved.

In my opinion, slavery in the United States was the most inhumane and crudest condition of human existence practiced anywhere else in the world. Yet, in spite of all the murders, the lynchings and beatings the slave had to endure were the absolute worst at eliminating of their humanity, culture, religion, and name. In the book and subsequent movie *Roots* by Alex Haley, Kunta Kinta, an African slave, refused to give up his ancestral name and accept the slave name of Toby. He finally gave in when he could no longer withstand the beatings he endured. To this day, most African Americans do not know what their true last name is.

Masters justified their treatment of the slaves because they were protected by law, given that the slaves were only considered as being 3/5 human. This situation gave the master absolute control over his slaves, even to the point of marriage between slaves and raising a family. But there was a problem. If the master allowed the slaves to marry in a traditional sense, under the law, the marriage would be legal. Also, with the marriage being legal and given that only humans married, the law would convey 100% humanity to the slave. Therefore, with the slave marriages being legal and the slave being 100% human, the masters could no longer break up the slave family due to legal and religious concerns. A new solution had to be adopted which allowed the slave to marry and remain in legal bondage. That solution came to be known as *jumping the broom.*

This ceremony was conducted by a slave elder who had no standing in the legal or religious communities. After a few words, had been said, he placed a broom on the ground in front of the bride and groom. At this point, they were required to jump over the broom in order to be considered married. To the slaves, they were married, but to the masters, in the eyes of the law and the religious community they were not. Problem solved. This condition led to the lack of strong black male role models throughout the ages who were able to counsel and guide young black children for generations.

As we proceeded in time during the 1950's and early 1960's, there were only two black men in history we were taught about, Booker T. Washington and George Washington Carver, one an appeaser the other a peanut researcher. Not very much to choose from, therefore, the only action heroes in our lives were white. This did not present a particular problem for us colored kids because when we adopted them as our heroes, skin color sort of faded away. Therefore, on Mardi Gras day I could be seen along with my posse riding my horse which was an old broom constructed in such a fashion to resemble a horse, riding around the neighborhood keeping an eye on Tommy as he flew over it. On this one particular day, we were allowed to party together, roam each other's neighborhoods without fear of being stopped by the police and generally have a good time until midnight when it all had to come to an end. Sadly, Jim Crow returned one second after midnight.

The effects of the Jim Crow laws were primarily directed at African American adults. The children were affected by those laws through their parents. They taught us what we could and could not do under the segregationist system that engulfed the city. I learned from a very early age to respect the law regardless if that law was good or bad because it was still the law. For instance, I was never to enter an establishment with a sign which stated, "WHITE ONLY". As a child, I could never understand why that was so, but my parents did, and I never disobeyed my mother. I was taught never to look at a little white girl with a smile on my face or in a suggestive manner. When responding to adults, white or black, *yes sir, no sir, yes ma'am, no ma'am, thank you,* and *please* were the rules of the day. I still respond in the same fashion today.

I lived in New York, Brooklyn to be precise. While living there I witnessed many different situations in which I attempted to compare and contrast the life of a child now as opposed to that of a child when I was growing up. After intensive study, I concluded that the lives of a child in today's world is far more difficult than when I was growing up. The answer to that question may not sit well with the so-called civil rights leaders back then and even presently. Some may ask how that can be with all the racism and bigotry being the order of the day as it was during my growing up. It's a very intriguing question. The service to say as a black child growing up during that time I survived into adulthood a long with both of my friends. In today world, black children have to dodge gun violence on their way to school.

If I were asked if I would trade my childhood experience growing up in segregated New Orleans, with all the racism and bigotry associated with it, to grow up in a Brooklyn neighborhood or any neighborhood in the North, South, East or West in today's world, the answer for me would be NO! As inhumane and unjust as those racist, bigoted laws were, there was never a time when fear was a constant companion for me while growing up in my neighborhood. During those hot, humid Southern nights, I recall my mother leaving the windows open along with the front and rear doors to facilitate the circulation of fresh air throughout the house. Natural gas was used to cook and heat our homes during what we considered to be those long cold winter months. This required at least two windows to be partially open for ventilation. In today's world, there is no way this practice would be considered while living in any large metropolitan area unless you live in a high-rise apartment building above the third floor. Also, all doors leading to the exterior would be locked using a deadbolt system, and all windows would have steel bars attached to keep people in, and most importantly, keep people out. In some cases, that included the fire department.

Other factors which contributed to the stability of my neighborhood, even under those dire circumstances, were the extended family and a stable home life, a father in all the homes to the best of my recollection, obedience to parents and other adults, neighborhood schools, religion, very limited television viewing and no video games. There were other factors, but I believe I have made my point. Nevertheless, there was a sadness in our lives that I, along with my friends, could feel from time to time as we went about our daily lives. One afternoon as we were sitting atop the shed on the roof, our usual meeting place, Jason begin speaking about a subject we rarely talked about.

As Jason begins to speak, the rest of us became very quiet and attentive. We could feel the seriousness in his voice. He spoke about how his family had planned an outing at the

Jim Crow Did Not Exist in my Backyard

Audubon Zoo the past Saturday. Jason's mom, Miss Barbara as she was known in the neighborhood, told him to ask Miss Helene if Tommy could join them. Then something surprising came out of Jason's mouth. He asked his mom if he could ask my mom if I could join them too. Her answer was no. He explained to her that I was his friend too, yet her answer was still no. When he asked why, she explained to him that Audubon Zoo was for whites only, the same way his school and most of the movie theaters were. She asked him if he remembered when she took him to the hospital a few months ago, to which he replied yes. She asked if he recalled seeing any colored people in there. He thought for a moment and then replied no. That's because the hospital is for white people only. Then he asked her if he should remain friends with us, to which she replied yes. However, she admonished him that colored and white people do not mix socially in public. They must remain separated in all things public because that is the law. According to Jason, his mom stated that she did not agree with it, but the law was the law until it changed. Change was in the air. However, it was a slight breeze instead of the hurricane forced wind which would take place a few years later.

We were all good friends, but we knew where the lines

were drawn. Yet, as opposed to the city, the lines in our neighborhood were blurred and no one seemed to care as long as we did not do anything stupid.

To all the kids in the neighborhood, the second-best holiday in the world next to Christmas was the 4th of July. Other than Mardi Gras this was the most public of all public holidays in the city. Everybody took part in the celebration either by going to the beach or backyard barbecues. In my household, we did both. Some holidays we went to the beach, and other holidays we would stay at home, and my father would build a swimming pool in our backyard. He would begin to construct it early in the morning because it took some time to fill it. Naturally, I was up with him. Once the pool was filled, my friends began to show up in their swimsuits, ready to take the plunge.

One of the strangest activities we had on the 4th of July was the backyard barbecue. It may not sound strange, but it's true. Almost everybody in the neighborhood barbecued either in the front yard or backyard. My father did the cooking while my mother prepared the meat, made the potato salad, candied sweet potatoes, and other goodies. Now, here is the strange part. My parents along with other parents in the immediate neighborhood cooked a huge amount of food. At least it looked that way to me. Some of our neighbors who did not cook were invited to come and receive a plate of food, and when I say a plate of food, I mean a plate of food. A short time later, other neighbors would show up bringing with them food platters. They would place their food platters on the kitchen table, engage in some small talk with my mother, receive their food platter from my mother and depart.

In the afternoon, when we grew tired of swimming, my mother made food platters for Jason and Tommy to take home to their parents and, in return, their parents would send food platters to us. I had never seen or tasted so much of the same food cooked in so many different ways. It was all good. Now I would be a fool to think that racism did not exist in my neighborhood at that time. However, I do believe that because of the activities my parents and other parents engaged themselves in, racism and bigotry were reduced.

Although Jim Crow did not exist in my backyard, it definitely existed in the Catholic Church. They were a willing participant in the racism and bigotry directed at the African American community. I can recall seeing Catholic priests and

nuns marching in protest, holding hands singing we shall overcome, and at the conclusion of the march go back to their segregated congregations and schools to minister and teach. I have
often wondered what was taught in those white Catholic
schools regarding the equality of mankind. Also, I wondered
why was it necessary to have two separate and unequal Catholic churches and schools.

The most loyal and faithful Catholics in the city of New
Orleans were African Americans, yet the church ignored our
plight as it related to civil rights. All Catholic churches,
schools, dioceses and fraternal organization were segregated.
The church I attended was St. Joan of Arc Colored Catholic
Church. What was strange about that church was its location. It
was located in a white community of the city, yet whites were
not a part of the congregation. Their church was located approximately one mile away. However, on some Sundays, a few
whites did attend mass at St. Joan of Arc church, yet they never
sat close to the altar, they segregated themselves towards the
rear entrance of the church. Unlike colored Catholics, who
were forced to segregate themselves in the rear of the church
while attending a white Catholic church, there the whites chose
to do it.

Jim Crow Did Not Exist in my Backyard

Other than race there was no difference between a colored Catholic church and its white counterpart. Yet, I was told that before a white Catholic attended mass at a colored Catholic church, he or she would contact their parish priest and inquire whether or not their Sunday obligation would be satisfied. All of the racism, bigotry, segregation and injustice directed at African American Catholics could have been eliminated with a stroke of the pen from the Archbishop.

If anybody knew anything about New Orleans, they would quickly come to the realization that the population was predominantly Catholic. From the mayor's office to the police and fire department, the vast majority of the men in charge of those organizations were Catholic. Therefore, the Catholic Church and the Archbishop reign supreme in the city of New Orleans. *Whatever you do unto the least of my brethren you do unto Me.* For generations, the Church has failed a large portion of its congregation. Change came to the Church, not willingly, but when it was forced to do so because of the changing circumstances of the time. I have never forgiven the Catholic church for its complicity and outright condoning of injustice directed at Colored parishioners.

Those feelings engulfed me later on in life. However,

[83]

as a child, I had no greater joy other than being Catholic and being in close contact with God. During my youth, I attended St. Joan of Arc Colored Catholic School. After enrolling, I applied to become an altar boy. I was accepted, and soon thereafter my training began. In some respect, training to become an altar boy was more difficult than training to become a United States soldier. It required deep study and concentration; I did both. We learned the Latin mass and all the responses to the priest while serving mass. It took a lot of studying; however, I mastered all of it. Many of the residents of New Orleans were Catholics, including Jason and Tommy. The rest of my friends were predominantly Baptist.

Religion in my family, and the majority of other families in the neighborhood took center stage in family life, regardless of the denomination. To obey and love the Lord was never a question, but a way of life. At a very young age, we learned and obeyed the Ten Commandments and never questioned any dogma relating to faith. Today, I do not question those tenants as it relates to my faith in God and His teachings. I question my faith in man as he interprets God's teachings. Yet back in those days the Catholic Church was the absolute center of my universe.

Jim Crow Did Not Exist in my Backyard

Tommy and Jason were experienced altar boys at their church. They had a few years on me because their parents enrolled them in Catholic school at the kindergarten level whereas I enrolled at the fifth-grade level.

While the Catholic Church was separate and unequal, there was one quality which could be shared by Catholics all over the world, consistency of the mass and the consistency of church teachings. While blacks were allowed to attend some white churches, they were not allowed to share 100% in the celebration of the mass. We went to mass in their church and immediately departed at its conclusion. There was no fellowship between black and white church members. Yet the exact same mass was celebrated in my church as well as theirs. This was why I looked to Jason and Tommy for help as I began my studies to become an altar boy.

Some afternoons we would meet on my back porch, and they would assist me with my studies. Each of us would have a book known as a missal. This is a liturgical book which contained all instructions mid texts necessary for the celebration of mass all over the world.

One afternoon while we were studying, Tommy asked

if he could see my missal. As he examined both books, a surprised look appeared on his face. He said they were exactly the same word for word, "So what?" I asked. Then he said something that surprised me.

"Your missal is for Coloreds, and my missal is for Whites, but it does not say that. Why?"

I told him I didn't know. As I look back, I think that was the moment when Tommy and Jason realized that there was no difference between Black Catholics and White Catholics. Thus there is no difference between the human families based on skin color.

Yet, the Catholic Church continued its racist policies for decades. As much as I loved the Church and as much as I wanted to be a part of it, there was always something deep within which said to me that I would never be considered a complete Catholic as long as my skin was black. I never reconciled with the Catholic Church and I never will. I found my true home in the Black Protestant Church and its teachings of the Black Liberation Theology, the same type of liberation the Bible taught in the book of Exodus and the same type of liberation theology taught by Jesus Christ. But the politics of the Church and time did not concern me right then. All I wanted to

Jim Crow Did Not Exist in my Backyard

do was be the best altar boy I could.

We didn't play very much in Jason's and Tommy's backyard, not because we couldn't, there was just not very much there which peaked our interest. There was a few small trees and shrubs plus because of the way their yards were situated; they were small compared to mine or Elmon. Therefore, my yard became the meeting place.

On this one afternoon, Tommy was helping me study my alter-boy lessons. He knew the mass backward and forward; he knew all the moves and prayers the priest said, the responses the altar boys made in response to his moves, and prayers. When we finished studying the lesson we began to role play with Tommy acting as the priest. My back porch in my backyard had three steps descending from it. Tommy stood on the second step, and I knelt on the third. It was not mandatory for us to understand everything the priest was saying. However, we had to recite the correct response to whatever he said. This is not to say we did not learn what he was saying, we did. This was accomplished by repartition. The mass never changed no matter what the circumstance and the wording was consistent as it relates to the responses of the altar boy. Plus, we used the movements of the priest and his position in order

[87]

to give the correct response.

Tommy stood there with hands folded in the praying position with head bowed. Then he began to speak; *humana, humana, humana, Humana.* Right then and there I knew Tommy had no idea of what the priest was saying, yet it was not a problem because I knew what the correct response was based on what he said and his position. It must be remembered that the mass was said in Latin. Therefore nobody knew what the priest was saying.

We did this for about half an hour when I noticed something strange. A few of our friends were sitting on the roof of the shed laughing themselves to tears. In my community, there were many black Catholic families as well as many black Protestant families. It just so happened that in my neighborhood most of my friends were Protestant. As they sat there, they begin to make jokes about what we were doing, and kids can be brutal at times. However, one of the funniest incidents which took place while we were engaged in our priest-altar boy reenactment involved my dog, Blackie. As we were reciting our prayers, Blackie came over and sat by me and begin to howl as if he was praying along with us.

Jim Crow Did Not Exist in my Backyard

Then I heard someone say, "I wonder if God understands dog." My backyard erupted into laughter including Blackie as he howled even more. As I was laughing, I wondered if God really understood dog. He had to, I thought, because I loved my dog very much and by his reaction to me, I could tell he loved me and God is love, and the love of God is given to all living things as I was taught. At the conclusion of our study session, we became involved in the serious business of playing, and we began a game of touch football.

As young children, I believe that God kept a close eye on us. He never let us feel the sting of racism or the bigotry of Jim Crow laws. This is not to say that I did not know that racism existed. Each Sunday, my father, would gather the family together for our weekly family drive. Other than my father, my family included my two older sisters and older brother. I was the baby at that time. My mother informed my father she wanted to visit our relatives in Edgar, Louisiana. Edgar is a small town located on the west bank of the Mississippi River, and it is the birthplace of my mother. We were excited to visit our relatives in Edgar because they lived on a large farm. On some occasions, we would spend a portion of our summer vacation there.

Joseph M. Moore

Another high point of our trip for me was driving across the Huey P. Long bridge. It was the biggest structure I had ever seen. Sometimes as we drove across the bridge, a train would be motoring along right beside us. Once we descended off the bridge, we had to drive through a number of little towns and hamlets. We were all singing along with my father and mother when suddenly everyone became quiet except me. I saw the anguish appear on my father's face as he looked out the window and I noticed my mother placed her arm around his shoulder which seem to relieve him somewhat.

As I looked out the window, I saw this large cross which had been burned in the front yard of this little farm house. He said that was the cross of the Ku Klux Klan. They are white people, and they don't like colored people. I asked why but he said nothing. We drove in silence all the way to our relatives' farm. We intended to remain there well into the evening but, when my father noticed the sun becoming heavy in the evening sky, he gathered us up, and we headed to the safety of our home.

The next time I saw Jason and Tommy I asked them if they liked me and our colored friends, to which they answered yes. They wondered why I had asked such a question. I then asked if they had ever heard of the Ku Klux Klan. They answered no and wanted to know who they were. I told them that my father said they were a group of white people who didn't like colored people. "Why?" they asked. I said I didn't know. With that, we shrugged off the issue. It didn't seem that important to us, so we went about the business of being kids.

Every time I think about my mother frying chicken, to this day my mouth begins to water. Frying chicken in my neighborhood was a science as the bird was being prepared and an art form as it was being cooked. As I look back, I realize how the soul went into soul food, or at least as it relates to my mother. As my mother would be frying her chicken, she would be singing some old negro gospel songs with an occasional hallelujah thrown in for good measure. As we sat down and blessed the table, I could taste God's hand as I took my first bite of that chicken. In my neighborhood, the Lord played an important role in the all of our lives. Therefore, if my mother was cooking her chicken in that manner, then it stands to reason that other mothers were doing the same thing.

Right across the street from my house lived Mr. and Mrs. Light along with their three children, Lenny, Terrance, and Kathy. Like I stated previously, frying chicken in my neighborhood was a science and an art. Therefore, every kid in the neighborhood loved eating it except for one, Terrance. He could not stand the stuff. As a matter-of-fact, he hated eating fried chicken so much when he took a bite it made him sick, and we knew that. So, every time his mother would fry chicken it seemed like every kid in the neighborhood would congregate on Terrance's porch waiting for a piece of chicken. Who said life didn't have its little perks?

We also received wisdom and knowledge from those little perks. When the city authorities, in an attempt to stifle our learning, our environment gave us the wisdom whether explicit or implied to adjust, adapt and overcome. This meant using our brain in a logical manner to achieve what was being denied to us educationally. Case in point one of the greatest quarterbacks in the National Football League is Payton Manning. One day I was watching TV, and Mr. Manning appeared in a TV commercial for a certain product. He was sitting at the counter eating a sandwich when an employee walked by and slipped onto the floor. He looked down at him as he laid on the floor saying "get up" and "rub some dirt in it". I thought for a while and said to myself that the expression sounded familiar. It brought me back to a time when that was exactly what we did when we scraped our knees and shins.

What I mean to say is we kept on playing in the dirt, in the muddy water without ever getting any type of infection, and we would let the wound heal on its own. When we scraped our knees, or legs, we did not head to the doctor's office like in most cases with kids and parents today. We went under the house to find spider webs to place on our wounds. If they were bleeding spider webs contain a unique substance which coagulated blood and stopped the wound from further bleeding. This along, with other knowledge helped us to survive in a world which did not care if we survived or not.

As children, back then, we believed in our own invincibility in much of the same fashion as today's kids. For example, we would run and jump on the rooftops of the small shed and the garage, never once thinking about falling off, and we never did. At other times, we would sit on the railroad tracks waiting for a train to come by and if it was moving slowly, we would jump on. When it sped up, we would jump off, never once thinking about the danger involved with this activity. However, all of that changed for me on this one day.

When I was in third grade, it seemed as if the universe was open to me, or so I thought. In it, there was nothing I could not do. On this one particular day, we were all in the school yard enjoying recess. I attended James Weldon Johnson Elementary School. It was located just one block from my house. As I look back, I am so glad that busing was not a policy invoked to achieve desegregation in schools or at least my school. I was perfectly happy with the school I attended. I don't think that the parents in my neighborhood would have liked it very much if their children had been bused to a school miles away from their homes in a white neighborhood.

Naturally, we attended segregated schools, and it was one of the few times we were not with our white friends. However, I guess recess was enjoyed by them as much as we enjoyed it. Recess was a time for kids to unwind from the stress of the classroom. It was a beautiful morning with the sun being high in the sky. It seemed like every kid in the school was in the schoolyard enjoying recess. My best friend Elmon and I were playing tag with other friends. Suddenly, I felt the urge to relieve myself. In other words, I had to go pee. When I walked into the boy's bathroom, I observed two boys facing off with each other with a crowd yelling, *"Hit him! Hit him!"*. *As* I stood in the doorway and soaked in all that was going on, I began yelling the same discourse. We kids always enjoyed watching a good fight. As I stood in the doorway, I placed my hand on the door-jam nor realizing I was placing myself in a vulnerable position. Suddenly I felt a surge of pain beginning in my hand then traveling throughout my body.

I looked at my hand, and I saw blood coming from everywhere, or so I thought. The door had slammed shut on my pinky finger cutting off the tip just below the cuticle. I bolted out of the restroom and ran frantically throughout the yard screaming at the top of my voice. Elmon and some other kid caught up with me and took me to the principal's office where my mother was called. The next people I recall seeing were my mother and father. They rushed me to the hospital, and the doctor stitched up my finger. He admitted me to the hospital for an overnight stay.

While in the hospital, I recalled how good the food was. There was this special dish they cooked for the kids call Boney Stew. It was a concoction made with tomato sauce, some type of meat, green peas and noodles. It was delicious. I told my mother how much I enjoyed it, and somehow she acquired the recipe because she cooked it for me often and it was better than the hospital's. The next day I went home.

Joseph M. Moore

When I arrived home, my house was filled with neighbors. There was food and soft drinks everywhere. All of my friends brought me little gifts like candy bars or cookies. We laughed and joked about how funny I looked running around the schoolyard like a chicken with its head cut off. Jason and Tommy were laughing and saying they wished they could have been there to see that. That was one of many little heartbreaks resulting from segregation. I stayed out of school for about a week. I told my mother I was ready to go back the next day, but she wouldn't hear of it. That was the most boring week of my life because all of my friends were in school and I had no one to play with.

After I had healed up, things went back to normal except for one minor change. I became a celebrity of sorts because they all wanted to see my chopped off finger as they referred to it, especially the girls.

In 1956, my baby sister was born, Linda Marie Moore, and she became the apple of my father's eye. At the time, my father was sixty-two and still one hell of a man. For a son, I adored him. He made my life complete, and he had that effect on all the kids in the neighborhood, but he was mine. My mother loved him beyond measure. He was her honey and Jo-

Jim Crow Did Not Exist in my Backyard

Moe when she became a little peeved with him. Before my mother and father were married, she had a daughter from a previous relationship, Victoria Marshall. Of all the sisters up to the time of her death from a childhood condition, we were the closest. Victoria was four years old when my mother and father married, therefore, she became my father's baby daughter, and he spoiled her beyond measure. God, what I would give to go back to that time in my life.

I along with my other siblings celebrated the birth of our baby sister along with our parents. Yet, something was very wrong in our household. Family members and some of our neighbors seemed to take more of an interest in the daily life of our family. Being a small child, I had no idea of what was about to devastate my life and totally impale the life of my mother.

Small children do not absorb critical information about their home-life, their environment and the world in which they live in much the same manner as most older people would. However, they picked up on certain key bits of information which cannot be ignored. When we brought my sister home from the hospital, there was jubilation throughout the neighborhood welcoming the new little addition.

Joseph M. Moore

One tradition which is uniquely Southern is when an event occurs at the home of a neighbors, no matter if it's good or not so good, a group of neighborhood mothers will arrive at that neighbor's home bringing gifts and turning the kitchen into a food lover's heaven. The aroma was hypnotizing it smelled so good. There would be greens, fried chicken, red beans and rice, Louisiana hot sausage, crawfish and cakes and pies of all types. There are not many other places in the country where neighbors get together in this fashion unless there are Southern folks.

According to my mother and other relatives my father had not been feeling well for some time. I never noticed it. All I saw was him getting up before the sun rose to go to work.

I always saw him as a strong, robust man doing what he had to do in order to maintain his family. Then one day my father went to the VA Hospital, and he did not come back home for a while. He had been going to the hospital off and on but not staying for an extended period of time. This time it was different. I had no idea what was wrong with him, but I could tell by the mood in my home that it was not good.

Then one day my mother came to me and stated that she and my oldest sister, Marion, were going to the hospital in order to bring my father home. I became very excited thinking I was getting my Honey back. Swimming pool in the backyard, money under the house, my friends and I climbing onto the truck eating ice chips and most of all just enjoying the love and attention my father gave to me all the time. It was coming back.

When the car pulled up in front of the house, and my father got out, I hardly recognized the man I called Honey. He had lost a tremendous amount of weight, and his clothes were hanging on him. He was bent over, and my mother and sister were on each side of him helping him walk. However, he was still wearing his signature white straw hat which he wore all the time. When I saw that I thought to myself, that's my old man.

I was standing on the front porch when the three of them walked passed me without saying a word. I followed them into the house, watched as they gently lowered him onto the bed. I wanted to go in and say something, but my mother said not to, let him rest for a while. There was a steady stream of people coming in and out of my house, but no one said very much, just a simple nod of the head. A few days later my father was taken back to the hospital. That was the last time I saw

[99]

him alive. My Honey was gone.

After the death of my father, the neighborhood was never the same as far as I could tell. As time went on, a reasonable amount of normalcy began to replace grief, except for my mother. I still played with my friends, we flew our kites, ate fruit from the fruit trees, picked pecans as they fell to the ground and did all the things we did in the past with one exception there was no more Mr. Joe to share it all with.

My mother continued to work. She was a cosmetologist. She styled and cut hair in her home shop set up by my father. It can be said that she was the only person in our family to have graduated college up to that point. Now, unlike in the past, my time was split between going to school, playing with my friends and babysitting while my mother worked. I didn't mind babysitting. I sort of liked playing with my sister, making her laugh and holding her while feeding her. As I thought about it over the years, my relationship with my sister soothed the pain of missing Honey. We held on as long as we could to the house my father provided, but it could not last. My mother could not maintain the rent along with all the other liabilities she was responsible for. We had to move.

In 1958 my mother informed me that we were going to

move out of the only neighborhood I had ever known. She said she was applying for public housing with the hopes of moving into the Lafayette projects in the seventh ward of the city. At that time the Lafayette project was the most sought after public housing unit in the city among blacks. It was within walking distance from Canal Street, the main shopping area in the city, and it was right across the street from the most famous black restaurant in the city, Dooky Chase. It was a mixed neighborhood in terms of not white people but black people. There were black people who looked black, black people who looked white and all the many colors in between. However, there was one negative element associated with that neighborhood, racism directed at blacks from blacks.

I can remember on one occasion I was a junior in high school dating one of our cheerleaders. We had made plans to attend the movies the following weekend. At that time, I was a skinny kid, about 5'10 inches tall weighing 130lbs. When I arrived at my date's home, I rang the doorbell and a tall, very light-skinned man with brown wavy hair appeared. He did not say anything to me as he looked me over from head to toe. My date came to the door introduced me to her father kissed him on the cheek and said see you later. As we walked away, he yelled out to me, "Young man," at which time I turned around facing him saying, "Yes sir." Then he said something very strange. "You just made the cut." I looked at him with a bewildered look on my face. He continued, "If you were one shade darker I would not let you go out with my daughter."

My date and I walked away, and I asked what all that was about. She said her father did not allow her to go out with dark skinned colored boys. Looking back, many times I had hoped she had married a black man so dark he could not be seen during the daytime let alone at night just to get back at her father.

As we waited for the public housing authorities to get back with us, we slowly began packing our belongings in anticipation of moving. We were told it could take a few months to a year to receive an answer. We were also told we would be given a choice of three housing facilities, of which we were offered the one we did not choose, The Desire Housing Project. It was considered the worst of all the facilities. If we refused, we were told we would not be considered for another facility. My mother accepted. In my opinion, it was one of the best decisions she ever made.

The Desire Housing Project was located in the in the

[102]

upper ninth ward of the city. The ninth ward at that time was predominately black, predominately poor and predominately neglected by the city as it related to some other wards. The ninth ward was divided into two sections, the upper ninth and the lower ninth located across the Industrial Canal. Criminal activity in the ninth ward was very high with the Desire Project leading the way. However, from the time we moved into the project during the latter part of 1958 up until I joined the United States Air Force in 1966, I can honestly say I never experienced any crime directed towards me or my family. I never saw any violent activity occurring during that period either.

Finally, the day had come for us to move. It was extremely sad for me because I had to leave my dog, Blackie, behind. The housing authority did not allow pets in its facilities. I asked Elmon to take care of Blackie for me, and with that, I hugged all my friends, kissed Blackie and departed with tears in my eyes. For the first time in my life, I felt so alone.

My childhood days were quickly coming to an end. I could see and feel the changes occurring within my body. Because of the death of my father and my mother securing a job on the three to eleven shift, I had to assume the role of man of the house when my mom was at work. My mother taught me

[103]

how to cook, clean house, and wash and iron clothes. Plus, it became my responsibility to help raise my little sister.

In 1955, Mrs. Rosa Parks gave birth to the Civil Rights Movement in the United States by refusing to give up her seat to a white man on a Montgomery, Alabama city bus where she was arrested. In New Orleans, during the decade of the 1950's there was no such thing as a Civil Rights Movement, and if there was the black community did not know of it. However, in my former neighborhood and being children we always considered ourselves as equal because there was no one around telling us we weren't in a language we could understand. Yet, with age comes wisdom and knowledge and, in some cases, sorrow. This phenomenon became quite evident the moment we moved into the Desire Project.

The first thing I noticed about the area was its racial makeup. It was 100% black, 100% isolated, 100% poor, and 100% neglected by the city authorities. It was as if they had taken the majority of the black population, put them in this one area and pretended they didn't exist, out of sight out of mind. Going into the project from the front were three sets of railroad tracks we had to maneuver around individually or by car in order to get in or out. I was used to being around railroad tracks and trains, however, this was a little different. The trains in my old neighborhood usually traveled at a slow speed, yet in my new neighborhood, they went so fast it was as if they were trying to break some type of speed record.

At the rear of the project, the same condition regarding the trains and railroad tracks existed. I can remember riding in the car with my mother and being stop at the railroad track at the entrance to the project because of a stopped train blocking the exit. We waited and waited for it to move but it didn't, and my mother decided to exit at the rear of the project. Once there, the same condition existed, a stopped train blocking the exit. We were trapped. In much the same fashion this condition repeated itself a few years later.

On September 9,1965 Hurricane Betsy smashed into New Orleans with wind gusts of 145 mph. This caused massive flooding in the area of the Desire Project. We couldn't get out unless there were boats available, which there weren't. We were trapped again. Now Jim Crow decided to engulf itself in the horrendous situation. Approximately four to five days passed before those of us in the project started to receive aid from the city or federal government. Yet, after the situation of flooding subsided and people were able to move about, word had gotten back to us that the Red Cross and other relief agencies were in the white neighborhoods in the surrounding areas giving aid and evacuating people. I am sure that situation led to the deaths of people in my neighborhood, all because Jim Crow decided to engage its segregationist racist laws at a time when it was not needed.

The ninth ward was the poorest and least affluent of all the wards in the city. In this neighborhood in which I found myself in, I can honestly say that Jim Crow had moved into my backyard. I justify that by pointing out how isolated we were and the fact that there was another housing project on the other side of the tracks, only this one was for whites and it was spotless. The fact that it was so clean was made obvious through the Desire Street city bus. We used this bus to travel into the center of the city for shopping or other errands. On its route, it had to travel through the white project, and we saw how clean it was and how the maintenance personnel maintained its upkeep.

In the case of the Desire Project, if it were not for the occupants keeping the place clean we would have been up to our necks in filth. However, I must say that as time went by things did improve and this improvement only came because of the pressure the Civil Rights Movement was beginning to exert.

In my old neighborhood, I never knew the true meaning of segregation. Reason being, I rarely traveled outside my neighborhood. Therefore, I didn't confront segregation head-on. I had always had white friends, and no one had ever told us we could not associate. I also had freedom of movement throughout my neighborhood. No one had ever told me I could not go here or there. Now things were very, very different. My new neighborhood was all black, and all of my new friends were black. Other than riding the buses, we were never to be in a white neighborhood, and that law was strictly enforced by the police.

On the flip side of that coin, I really never wanted to be in a white neighborhood. My friends being all black were of no consequence because I am black. The fact that I had white friends was a situation of circumstance, not a situation of encouragement. Although school integration is a way of life now, I never had any problems attending segregated schools. All of the black kids that I knew, including me, did the very best we could with what we had to work with. The only reason why I supported school integration was because of the fact that white kids were getting the best of what the city had to offer and black kids were getting hand-me-downs. The issue went far beyond not socializing or mingling with whites. If the city could have guaranteed me separate and 100% equality in all things, I would have been happy with that.

As the decade of the 1950's was drawing to a close and the decade of the 1960's was opening, I found myself still in Jim Crow's backyard, yet things were changing. I was on my way to high school. The high school I chose or I should say the high school which chose me was St. Augustine High School.

St. Aug, as we referred to it, was one of the top high schools in the city, black or white. Its academic program was second to none, and its extra-curricular programs were some of the best in the city. Yet, it was still a segregated high school in the city, even though the US Supreme Court had ruled that segregated schools were unconstitutional. However, be that as it may, I would not have attended another high school, black or white other than St Aug.

Once my family moved into the project and we had settled in I never felt so alone as I did the first month there. We had heard so many bad things about the project that my mother refused to let me go outside to play and meet a new friend for a while. But, things got better. Our neighbors began showing up at our door with welcoming gifts or just stopping by to say hello and introduce themselves. They often brought their children with them and, as a result, I made new friends. Soon thereafter I was out, and about exploring my new backyard and, believe me, it was a hundred percent different than my old backyard.

My community and neighborhood were completely black. It was as if the authorities gathered up most of the black citizens and dumped us in the ninth ward and forgot about us. Nevertheless, things were changing. Dr. King's work and ministry *as it* related to the Civil Rights Movement was beginning to take on a momentum of its own and black people were beginning to feel empowered for the first time when dealing with the city. But, there was still an extremely long way to go.

In my old neighborhood, separation and segregation were never really felt as a real problem for the kids. But, in this new environment, a complete transition took place. I no longer came in contact with white people on a friendly basis or on any other basis. For the entire time, I lived in the project all of my playmates and friends were black and because of that I began

[109]

to form new ideas and prospectives on the true meaning of being black. Yet, when I crossed those tracks to enter my neighborhood, it was as if giant doors closed preventing me from seeking my true destiny.

The good thing about being raised in the Desire Housing Project, in my opinion, outweighed the few negative aspects of growing up there. Yes, there was crime there, but thanks to my mother and my Aunt Rose and our religious upbringing, I avoided those situations in which I could have placed myself in jeopardy and also I was rarely out and about at night due to the fact that I was responsible for my baby sister.

As time went by, I began to make more and more new friends as my teenage years were being thrust upon me. As I grew older, my knowledge of civil rights, or the lack thereof, increased. I began to notice things I hadn't noticed in the past, such as why there were no black city-elected officials. Why was my neighborhood neglected when it came to city services such as police, fire and ambulance services, slow garbage pickup and street cleaning, recreation and city-sponsored activities for young people? The answer was plainly clear: NO POLITICAL POWER!

Jim Crow Did Not Exist in my Backyard

The poll tax and literacy test were still in place in order to keep blacks from the polls, and the grandfather clause was still in use to maintain the white voting majority. I never saw a candidate for political office campaign in my neighborhood nor did I see any campaign signs. I can't recall to this day if I ever saw any voting facilities there. Furthermore, I never saw my parents or any other black parents going to vote or even discussing the issue. There was a reason for that called, "voter intimidation". Black people very rarely appeared in the local media, however, when a black person was lynched for attempting to vote or trying to get other black people to register it appeared all over the local media, indirect intimidation. The law didn't give us any relief, leaving us no other alternative but to take to the streets.

White politicians knew they did not need the black community to win elections due to the fact that there weren't that many registered black voters in the city. Those politicians never came to my neighborhood to preach their corrupt political ideology nor did they post campaign signs to promote themselves. Political corruption in Louisiana politics is an established fact, past and present. Also, the disenfranchisement of African Americans at the polls made political corruption more tolerable to the white electorate.

Another issue which affected my neighborhood was the convenience of shopping. There were no *mom and pop* grocery stores and the two markets in the area were dirty and the items sold were of poor quality and priced too high. The customers of those markets were all black. This meant that we had to gather the family in the car and travel for miles to the super-market where white people shopped in order to get good qual-ity food at a reasonable price.

As time went by and I got older, I began to experience Jim Crow segregation and racial isolation in such a way that I had never experienced in the past. I lost contact with my white friends and never made any new ones. On the other side of the tracks, there was a white housing project. Other than riding on the city bus, we never ever ventured into their neighborhood for two important reasons. First, it wasn't safe and second, it was illegal for us to enter.

When my family relocated, I felt as if the entire world was closing in on me because of the racism and bigotry di-rected towards me and others. It was as if one world ended and another had begun. For the first time in my life, I found myself in a completely isolated, segregated environment. Now that I had to travel some distance to and from school, I found myself being confronted by police officers just because of the neighborhood I was in or where I was waiting at the bus stop. All the Jim Crow rules were the same, but growing into adulthood meant they were enforced more emphatically. When I traveled outside of my neighborhood on the city buses as far as the white passengers were concerned, we did not speak to them nor did they speak to us. We did not sit next to each other. It was as if we were living on the same planet but in different dimensions.

In my old neighborhood, I was constantly around white people from playing on the levees with them to horsing around on the streetcar. From meeting up at the corner grocery store to just walking around the neighborhood. This was the way of life in my childhood environment. However, in my new community, there were times I did not see a white person for weeks, apart from the television of course. This situation existed in most black communities as it applied to children throughout the city. However, during all of the racial unrest throughout the country, I believe the one major element above all others which kept the city from exploding was the religious experiences shared by most of its citizens.

[113]

Joseph M. Moore

During the time of my youth, New Orleans was a very religious city. On any given Sunday, the churches were packed with parishioners and members thanking God for their daily bread. Yet most white Christians of the South, New Orleans included, would not invite a colored person to their dinner table in order to break bread with them.

When my childhood friends and I would get together to just sit around and talk, we would ask each other why we could not do that or why we could not attend the same schools or something simple as drinking from the same water fountain. The answer would always be the same; you are colored, and I am white, and that would be the end of it. Then we would do what kids normally do, play and have fun.

In my new world that same answer, "You are colored, and I am white," was no longer acceptable. Yes, all of the segregation laws were still intact. However attitudes among blacks, especially young black people were changing. We were no longer willing to accept the status quo. But what could we do about it? Not much. The change over from the decade of the 1950's to the 1960's occurred without any meaningful positive changes that affected the African American community. All of the Jim Crow apartheid laws from reconstruction to the present

[114]

remained in effect. The Civil Rights Movement was in its infancy without a single strong national leader. Finally, the laws which were designed to protect and serve all the citizens were often used to harass, intimidate and in some cases led to the murder of black citizens. We, the young black children, were not in a position to engage the city authorities, not just yet.

Racial segregation especially in the deepest parts of the South or, more specifically, in the gulf coastal states, regardless of the amount of time it had been in place was doomed to buckle under its own weight. It's like trying to prove a negative fact which is impossible or at the very least improbable. Along the coast of Texas, Louisiana, Mississippi, Alabama and Florida, the people and their cultures were so intermingled it became almost impossible to tell who was who. This phenomenon did not occur overnight; it began with the settlements of those states in the 17th and 18th centuries. Therefore, New Orleans, with its mixture of Africans, Europeans, Latinos, Native Americans and West Indians presented a problem. With the exception of Africans, Europeans, and West Indians, how could the others be classified? Were they white or black?

In the beginning, that was easy, either you were white or a slave. However, as time went by that question became more and more difficult to answer due to the influx of people from other countries. Now the issue of being white and looking white became a problem. Primarily, the problem was the slave master's own making. When the African slave trade became illegal, the slave masters along with his overseers took it upon themselves to produce slave children. At that point, the complexion of the plantation begins to change.

Case in point, the two families of Thomas Jefferson, the third President of the United States, his white family and his African slave family. As time proceeded to the modem era, a new solution was needed to solve the problem of who was white and who was not. The solution came to be known as The One Drop Rule.

The One Drop Rule can be defined as a person with a trace of African blood running through his or her veins is to be considered black. Therefore, if there is any doubt about the ancestry of a person who claimed to be white, it became that person's responsibility to prove he was actually white. Otherwise, legally, he or she was black.

During my freshman year in high school, there were some in the black community who could have passed for white, and I am sure many did. However, there was one student

Jim Crow Did Not Exist in my Backyard

who, if I were to see him on the street, I would have said he was white, no doubt in my mind. He had white hair, a white complexion, he spoke like a white person and, most importantly he looked every bit white except for one thing. He had large lips, and at the time, white people with large lips were not in fashion. Plus, it was considered an African trait. He told me that the hospital had made a mistake by putting a C on his birth certificate indicating "Colored". This student was extremely intelligent, more than I was, I must say, and because of that C, he was barred from attending the top white high schools in the city. Yet, what he did not realize at that time was because of that C he was forced to attend the top high school in the city and upon graduation he received a four-year academic scholarship at Massachusetts Institute of Technology.

Yet Jim Crow laws still produced a heavy burden on those black children going from childhood to preteen and teenagers. This burden began at the time of slavery up to and after the enactment of the Civil Rights Act of 1964. Education, not protesting for civil rights, was the most important factor in my family's life. My mother made sure that my education did not suffer just because Jim Crow segregation put up road blocks in front of me. She insisted that I did my homework every night and she checked to make sure it was done. In a, roundabout way she taught me that I the whole person was more important than the sum of my parts, and education was the only way I could break the chains of second class citizenship. Although she was right, I was becoming more and more impatient with those chains. I had to take an active role somehow without causing my mother pain. I loved her so very much.

Now that I was older, a young teenager in a new neighborhood and environment, I began to sense a new duty or mission being forced upon me. I had to do something and not just stand on the sidelines while some of my friends became engaged. As previously mentioned, I attended St. Augustine HS, administered by the Catholic Dioceses of New Orleans for African American young men. We, the black students of Catholic schools, had a dilemma. All of the schools within the Catholic school system were segregated, plus the Catholic Church did not take an active role in the Civil Rights Movement. Also, it did not adjust very well to negative public opinion directed against it. Therefore it maintained the "out of sight, out of mind" philosophy, and anyone who violated that strategy was cast aside. This included students engaged in civil disobedience. So, we had to develop a strategy.

Jim Crow Did Not Exist in my Backyard

What we did not want to do was bring attention to ourselves and the Catholic Church which could have resulted in expulsion from school. Yet, we wanted to be engaged in something bigger than ourselves in order to make a difference. What we decided was not to engage in civil disobedience overtly but engage covertly. For example, while riding the city bus, we would purposely sit next to a white person, and if there were no objections, we would continually sit there. If there was an objection or the bus driver got involved, which they rarely did, we would vacate the seat without objection. This strategy of engagement and peaceful disengagement when the situation demanded was being conducted all over the city by Catholic school kids. It told the racist government that we no longer wanted to sit behind those signs. Not much longer thereafter, the city buses were desegregated. But the change for both public and Catholic was slow in coming.

I cannot think of one single time during the Jim Crow era when the Catholic Church engaged itself in any substantial way to further the cause of civil rights. What I can remember was watching on television those nuns and priests marching with Dr. King singing, "We Shall Overcome." Yet, when the event was over, they would return to minister to their all white

parishioners and teach in their segregated schools. I cannot recall any nun, priest, or lay teacher protesting the racist segregationist policies of the Catholic Church nor did I ever see or
hear of the Catholic Church encouraging its people to do so.
From my teenage years, onward I became so disillusioned and
angry with the Church that I severed all ties with it. I still have
a great respect for the Church as being a place of prayer and
the house of the Lord; however, as for the men who are in
charge, I have no respect for them, many of whom are still
alive today. If I am wrong, I am sure God will forgive me
based on the Church's past practice.

The country was at a crossroads during the decade of
the 1960's, and I do not know how the United States of
America survived it. Extreme violence was the catch-word of
the day and my God, did the country live up to it. There were
over thirty-one major riots in the United States and most were
centered on race. However, those riots were not exclusive to
the South; they were spread all over the country, but the most
severe violence happened to occur in the

South. This decade was plagued with assassinations beginning with Medgar Evers, June 12, 1963—Civil Rights
Worker and Activist. September 15, 1963: Addie Mae Collins,

Jim Crow Did Not Exist in my Backyard

Cynthia Wesley, Carol Robertson and Denise McNair, the four little girls preparing to attend Sunday school when the church was bombed by a hateful white racist. November 22, 1963 John F. Kennedy—President of the United States of America, was assassinated. June 24,1964: Civil rights workers James Cheney, Andrew Goodman and Michael Schwemer was murdered on a desolate Mississppi country road. February 21, 1965: Malcolm X—Civil rights activist murdered due to the fact that his policies were contrary to that of the Nation of Islam. March 25, 1965: Viola Liuzzo—Civil rights worker murdered for giving a ride to an American Soldier who happened to be black. April 4, 1968: Dr. Martin Luther King, Jr—Civil Rights national leader, murdered. June 6, 1968: Robert F. Kennedy—Brother of the late President John F. Kennedy, Senator, and presidential candidate.

Those assassinations were only the tip of the iceberg, as compared to the protests and violence associated with the Vietnam war. The country was in dire straits and being ripped apart as a result of the war. This situation led to the end of President Lyndon B. Johnson's political career with his announcement not to run or accept his party's nomination for President of The United States.

[121]

Because of the Vietnam war, the country found itself at a crossroads between its domestic policies and its international interest. The political instability and social unrest within the United States had a far-reaching effect on the rest of the world, especially its enemies. For the first time in the Vietnam War, North Vietnam found a new ally, and that ally was public opinion and growing opposition by young people to the war. Violent protest to the war began to spread all over the country. Along with its counterpart, some civil rights protests turned violent as a result of police action against the marchers on the Edmund Pettis Bridge in Selma, Alabama on March 7, 1965. All of this gave the appearance that the United States was at war with itself, again.

North Vietnamese political and military leadership saw a great opportunity in order to take advantage of all the unrest affecting the United States. They knew they could not win a military victory against the United States. However a psychological victory was entirely possible.

On January 30, 1968, the Tet Offensive was launched over the entire country of South Vietnam. In Saigon, the US Embassy was attacked with limited success. However the enemy captured the embassy and held it for six hours until it was

[122]

Jim Crow Did Not Exist in my Backyard

retaken by US troops and embassy personnel. Over 35,000 enemy troops were killed along with over 4,500 allied soldier casualties, mostly American. Tet demonstrated to the American People that death and time were of no consequence, they would fight on forever if need be. This led news reporter Walter Cronkite to declare that the war was unwinnable and would be the downfall of an American President.

All of those events were occurring while I was a young teenager growing up in the Desire Project in segregated New Orleans. Not being able to sit down and eat a tuna sandwich at a lunch counter just because of the color of my skin seem infinitesimal as compared to what this country was going through. Yet the color of one's skin trumped all things as it related to interpersonal relationships between people in New Orleans and the South.

As time went by, it seemed like the grip of segregation increased. I say that to say I no longer came in contact with white people or at least in the way I interacted with them in the past. I never developed any new white friends. I began to feel the true meaning of segregation as Jim Crow intended for me to feel it: apartheid and the true isolation and separation of a people based solely on skin color. This was the true armor of

[123]

the white separatist movement. Yet even with all its armor, cracks began to develop.

As with Soweto in South Africa, the ninth ward became an unofficial black township. And like Soweto, it was very poor, very black and very neglected. There was nothing in the past the black community could fall back on while struggling to find its identity and its God- given right as full citizens of the city of New Orleans, the state and the country. Although some minor improvements had been made, the major problem facing the African American community was the idea of self and where we as a people fit in, in the overall scheme of things.

We got our answer from an unusual source, "The God-father of Soul", with his mega and historical hit song in January 1968 "Say It Loud - I'm Black, and I'm Proud" by Mr. James Brown. When I first heard that song, not only did it sound good, it made chills run up and down my spine as I am sure it did with the majority of black people. For the first time in our communal life as a people and an individual being called "Black" was not a derogatory term. Being able to accept ourselves for what we were and liking ourselves and not wishing we were somebody else was the first and most important nail

Jim Crow Did Not Exist in my Backyard

in the coffin of Jim Crow.

There was not very much for black children to engage in as far as recreation was concerned in the Desire Project. NORD, New Orleans Recreation Department, was more concerned with the activities related to white children than us. To my best recollection, NORD had no facilities in my neighborhood for us to enjoy. However, that situation was not particular to only my neighborhood; it was a fact in 99% of the black neighborhoods in the city. Plus, where one was found, it was separate and unequal.

Fortunately, the winds of change were blowing, slowly but surely. The city could not maintain its racist, discriminatory policies against its black citizens forever. This was due to the fact that the only thing constant in the universe is change and like it or not, change will happen. The next factor which affected change of those racist policies was money, and Louisiana politicians loved money and did not want any disruption in its flow.

New Orleans was a medium sized city in the United States. However it was one of the most recognizable cities by name in the world. Along with that title, the money flowed in.

What caused this monetary bonanza was the two-week celebration of Mardi Gras. Unlike cities in states like Mississippi which had no worldwide standing and no economic incentives, those people just did not give a damn. They would kill you for looking the wrong way. New Orleans was different. The flow of worldwide money into New Orleans treasuries kept the politicians living in their plantation-style homes in the most affluent section of the city, the Garden District.

Rumors began to spread all over the city that a major protest was being planned for the Mardi Gras festivities of 1962. It was said the civil rights workers from all over the country would converge on New Orleans to organize the event. Evidently, those rumors began to be heard by politicians and in time those rumors would be heard throughout the country and world. Also during that time period, we were being told that meetings were being conducted between the so-called black community leaders, business people, and the politicians. Although the Mardi Gras demonstrations never happened, everything did not remain the same.

In 1962, I was a sophomore in high school, and I rode the city bus to and from school. On this one particular day, while riding the bus, which happened to be crowded, there

[126]

were two white ladies sitting in the seats where I was standing. As the bus came to the bus-stop, one lady got up and departed leaving her portion of the seat empty. I continued to stand. There was a black lady seated behind the seat in question. She looked up at me and said, "Young man, you can sit there if you want."

Surprised by what she had said I replied, "No I can't. If I do, I will be arrested." I looked at the white lady whose face was beginning to turn red, thinking to myself that something was up. The black lady indicated to me that we could now sit anywhere on the bus and that it was the law now. I thought for a while as I noticed the white lady slide to the edge of the seat in order to prevent me from sitting. Then I did something I never thought I would do in my life, I forced myself past her and sat on that portion of the seat near the window. She got up and reported the incident to the bus driver. I began to get nervous with my hands becoming sweaty, wondering what I had gotten myself into as the bus driver stopped the bus and walked to where I was seated. He looked at me and then turned his attention to her saying the law had changed, and that we could can sit anywhere we wanted to on the bus. He informed her that she could sit back down, stand, or get off the bus. With that, he turned and resumed his bus route, and she departed the bus.

I was shocked. A new page had just been turned in my life, and I enjoyed every minute of it. As the days went by and I rode the city buses all over the city, I experienced another shock. All those degrading signs informing black people of where they could sit or could not sit on the bus were gone. The second nail in Jim Crow's coffin had been hammered in.

Changes in the city began to pick up a little speed, small changes at first but change none the less. For the young men of St. Augustine High School, the city bus was the perfect place to meet girls due to the fact that St. Augustine was an all-boys school. When we wore our school colors, purple and gold, accompanied by that big letter "A" across our chest, the girls seemed to flock to us. Even the white girls were giving us that look as if saying, "If only we could." That's just how popular St. Aug was throughout the city. Yet, before and after school, we were so preoccupied with that activity we did not notice what was really taking place throughout the city.

On my way home after school and while flirting with one of the female passengers, I saw a strange sight- a black man sitting in the driver's seat. I was shocked to see that. There were not that many passengers on the bus, so I sat right behind him and asked a few questions.

He informed me that the city had opened up jobs for black bus drivers, only a few right now and mostly in black neighborhoods in order to prevent culture shock in the white neighborhoods. They wanted to gradually introduce us in their neighborhood maybe one or two of us at a time and only on the night shift. But it was a beginning, he said. Imagine that, I thought. Not only can we sit anywhere we wanted, now we have black bus drivers driving us to where we wanted to go. "What is this world coming to?" I said laughing to myself.

The city gave in to some of the demands of the black community because they had no choice. If those demonstrations would have kicked off during Mardi Gras, they could have become violent and disruptive, causing chaos throughout the city with the loss of millions of dollars. All city services would have been impacted, and the business community would have been forced to close their doors. That Mardi Gras season was quiet. The locals, as well as visitors, shared in all of the festivities; all is separated, and unequal of course, and the money still flowed in. The city authorities were informed by the black community that this was the beginning, not the end.

Shortly thereafter, most city transportation services were integrated along with some lunch counters, hotels, and some other venues. However, schools, hospitals, recreational facilities, housing and other services remained segregated for years. Plus, when I along with my fellow community members crossed those tracks leading into the Desire Housing Project, it was as if we were the throw-away population of the city. All of the leadership of the city, including the so-called black leaders, forgot about us.

All of the families living in the Desire Housing Project were poor, including my family. All of us subsisted on some type of government welfare program. Today, June 2013, the national unemployment rate is 7.6%. In White America, it's 6.5% conversely in the African American community it's 13.5%. In this bountiful country, it is un-American for a group of people to have an unemployment rate so high. Considering what the unemployment rate for today's blacks are and considering what the unemployment rate for that same group would have been in the 1960's in the South, the system was designed to keep black families in poverty. At that time the only jobs available to us were chauffeurs *(Driving Miss Daisy)*, porters, busboys, waiters, dishwashers, and cooks and making between

Jim Crow Did Not Exist in my Backyard

$.50 and $1.00 an hour.

To the best of my recollection, my family never made use of food banks or thrift shops, The Salvation Army or The American Red Cross. WHY? We were fully aware of the segregationist policies directed toward us by the city, but what I could not understand was why would those organizations treat the families in the Desire Project as if we had some type of rare decease. They were nowhere to be found.

The prime directive of The Salvation Army, The Red Cross, and other like-minded organizations was and is to help families in times of need. The Salvation Army travels to the depths of the Amazon, the African continent, they combat wild animals, diseases, known and unknown and political unrest in order to spread the word and render help when needed. But to the families of the Desire Project a community in the city of New Orleans in the state of Louisiana in The United States of America, it was too dangerous and too black to venture into, so they didn't come to offer assistance. Be that as it may, what we didn't have we didn't miss. Therefore we made use of what we had with the assistance of my family and neighbors, unlike those organizations, who never turned their backs on us.

In spite of all the negative information available at the

[131]

time, living in the ninth ward in general and the Desire Project, in particular, I should have been either a pusher, addict, in prison, dead or all of the above, but I am not. Due to my childhood and formative upbringing by my mother, family members, and community while living in the project, I am a high school grad, I have a degree in healthcare science, I am a Certified Surgical Technologist, I am a Certified Surgical First Assistant, I am a published author, *Stories from The Back of The Bus,* published by Publish America, I am a Vietnam and United States Air Force veteran, and I have never been imprisoned in my life. All of that may sound good, but my story and I are not unique; millions have come out of the ghetto and went on to serve, giving credit to their families, their community, The United States and themselves for a job well done.

Yet, being able to achieve in an environment not dedicated to advance the goals of young black citizens was difficult in and of it. In order to achieve, my mother's instructions to me was to be better than the next person especially if that person was white. Just reciting the answers was not enough. I had to demonstrate the what, when, where, why and how I arrived at my conclusion. That was a difficult challenge, but the infusion of knowledge I was able to store for later use gave me the satisfaction of knowing what I learned may be just enough in order for me to accomplish my goals. All young black people had to do this because affirmative action wasn't even a dream at that time.

Yet, as isolated and shut off from the rest of the city as we were, there was safety in the ghetto because of its isolation. Once I crossed those tracks, I knew I would not be harassed by the police as opposed to other sections of the city, and I don't recall being stopped by the police in my neighborhood the entire time I lived there. The crime of burglary was kept to a minimum for four main reasons. First, there were no rich people or people of means residing in the project; we were all poor with very little worth stealing. Second, whenever strangers would appear in the immediate neighborhood, we would keep a close eye on them, day or night. Third, we lived so close to each other any strange noise would cause the neighbors to investigate. Finally, there was no real drug problem at that time. Therefore the constant need to replenish one's income to support a drug habit by stealing or other means had not reached epic proportions, yet.

I discovered my very first true love while living in the

project. Her name was Virgie, and she and I were the same age, 15. Her complexion was dark with long wavy jet black hair. We were about the same height, but she was beautiful and unlike mine her facial skin was blemish free. Somewhere in her ancestry, Native American blood ran through her veins.

This is true of many African Americans living in New Orleans and the South. Some of those slaves who were able to escape the bondage of slavery intermingled with the indigenous Native American people resulting in some beautiful brothers and sisters. We were constant companions. The only time we separated was during school hours. In the afternoon, she would visit me at my home due to the fact that after school I had to babysit my sister. We never engaged in any sexual intercourse because I was not sure how to do it and she told me she was not ready, so we only went so far and stopped.

For the first time as a young man, I learned what it felt like to love a woman and it felt good. One afternoon while we were sitting on the porch of my building, I said to her I was going to do something which would cause me to never forget her. She wanted to know what I was about to do, "It's a surprise" I informed her. Later on, in my bedroom, I retrieved a bottle of Indian ink from a drawer and drew an outline of a heart with an arrow going through it. From my mother's room, I found a needle and proceeded to jab myself over and over. It didn't hurt because I barely penetrated the skin. However, it allowed for the ink to set up just beneath the skin layer causing the tattoo to become permanent.

The next time I saw Virgie, I showed her what I had done. I told her that because of that tattoo she will always be in my heart and I will never forget her. She hugged and kissed me saying we will always be together. Well, our always be together lasted for about one year at which time her family moved, and I lost contact with her. However, to this day whenever I gaze upon that heart-shaped tattoo on my left arm, I think of my Virgie. I am just happy I didn't put her name in it. As far as others are concerned, only God and I know who my little heart represents.

As I have stated previously because of Jim Crow, the city invested very little funds if any for recreational activities for the people of the ninth ward. In front of my apartment was a big, open field containing trees and the elementary school my sister attended. I must say the maintenance people mowed the lawn on a regular basis. This allowed us to engage in our daily

baseball game. In the schoolyard, there were four interconnected basketball courts. However, Jim Crow public school
laws did not allow us to play basketball on school property after school hours. Other than our baseball game, the basketball
courts were the only other means of recreation we had. So naturally we hopped the fence and played or games.

From time to time the police would show up in a vain
attempt to chase us off the school's property, but we were prepared for them, we had lookouts. Whenever they saw them ap-
proaching, the lookouts would give a signal, and we would
scatter. That became a game in its own right. We did not fear
the police very much because of their rare presence in the
neighborhood and their half-assed attempt to remove us from
the courts. Once they left the area, we would resume our games
because we knew we would not see them in our neighborhood
for days or weeks at a time. Sometimes a rookie white officer
would show up and in order to impress his veteran partner he
would chase us around for a while. We feared him the most because as he chased us, he would have his hand on his weapon
and sometimes he appeared to remove it from his holster. After
a while, he would give up the chase. They never caught us.

Jim Crow Did Not Exist in my Backyard

Going swimming to cool off on those hot, muggy, summer days in New Orleans meant taking that long trip to Lake Pontchartrain. That was the only place black kids in the ninth ward could go to cool off and have some fun in the water. The only other body of water close to my home was the Industrial Canal. The canal was within walking distance from my home. However, it was a challenge to get there. Many of the open fields we had to walk through were overgrown with weeds and tall grass. Many contained abandoned cars and other large rusting fifty-five gallons sealed drums. We never knew what was in those drums, but they would not have been there if the EPA had been around at that time. However, in the ninth ward where ever there was abandoned overgrown property, illegal dumping could be found.

The Industrial Canal is a waterway which connects Lake Pontchartrain to the Mississippi River. One of the functions of the 5.5-mile waterway is flood prevention and protection for the city of New Orleans. It never worked. Hurricanes Betsy, Katrina, and Rita can attest to that fact. Also, the same thing will happen when another major hurricane attacks New Orleans.

When I look at pictures of the Industrial Canal and the

[137]

surrounding area, I always wonder where and what Industrial Canal those pictures refer to because it looks so pristine. In reality, the portion of the canal I am familiar with is far different than what was being portrayed. When our walk was coming to an end while walking through those abandoned fields, we knew we were getting close to the canal because we could smell it. The smell was that of decaying garbage, flesh, and chemicals combined. On those hot, humid days with little or no wind blowing the smell would be so pervasive we would close all the windows except for a few centimeters for ventilation and turn on all the fans we had to keep cool.

After crossing some railroad tracks and dirt roads, we finally reached our destination. On the shoreline of the canal were several old rusting ships being dismantled for scrap iron by crews. As the pieces were cut away, they would fall into the water for later retrieval. With all of those rusted and cutaway sections underneath and floating on top of the water, it gave the appearance that the water was rusting itself. Also, there would be oil slicks in the water along with what I considered to be bags of floating garbage passing by. It was sometimes said that bodies were dumped there. It was also said that people and industry used the canal as a dump site. From what I have seen, I

Jim Crow Did Not Exist in my Backyard

believe it. We did not go near the water; my mother forbade me from even thinking about going into that water and naturally, I obeyed. Yet, we lingered there for a while watching the crews dismantle the ships and watching those heavy sections fall into the water giving off a loud-sounding splash. Not long thereafter we left.

My mother's sister lived in the lower ninth ward. In order to reach my aunt's home, we had to cross the Industrial Canal via a bridge. As we crossed the bridge, I could see children playing in that dirty water. I have always prayed that they grew up healthy. I missed my backyard swimming pool built by my father.

As I recall, two of the major disappointments while residing in the project was the loss of the neighborhood playground unknowingly provided by the city and the loss of my white friends from whom I learned some of the secrets of humanity which Jim Crow tried to prevent me from learning. From 1959 to 1966, the years I lived in the Desire Project, I disassociated myself from all white people even though the experiences from my younger days with white people wasn't bad. I didn't acquire any new white friendships or socialized with them in any way. As far as the neighborhood playground was concerned, my roaming adventures with my friends, white and black, was over. I had to make do with what was presented to me. It wasn't much. However, it wasn't that bad. Other than traveling to and from school, I did not stray very far from home. It was not necessary because that large open field in front of my home with its shade trees and well-kept lawn presented me with new opportunities I had never experienced before, *girls.*

I was getting older now, going into my mid-teenage years. The old childhood games I had engaged in were over now. I had crossed the threshold of puberty and looked at girls and young women in a completely different way. In the late afternoon, just before a complete disappearance of the sun, some of my friends and I would lie on the grass under those trees a discuss those things which were important to us: sports, school, and girls. Sometimes a group of girls would join us and engage in our conversation. A young man could not ask for anything better than that. As we sat there and talked, I found myself staring at this one particular young lady. She would look at me from time to time, smile and turn away, yet I felt a connection. One of my friends observed me staring at her, tapped me on the shoulder, asking me if I was going to say anything to her. I didn't know what to say; I was speechless, and I could not think of a word to say. I just looked at her. Finally, she broke the ice by saying her name was Sharon. She was one of the many girls I became friends with while living in the project. From a personal standpoint, ghetto life was not that bad. Yet those Jim Crow Laws not only hurt and caused harm to those white people who did not assent to them it hurt and caused harm to those very same people perpetrating those hateful laws against those living in the shadow of freedom, only they were too ignorant to realize it.

Jim Crow laws, racism, and segregation were responsible for the death of numerous African Americans. During its heyday, those who perpetrated those crimes were all white men associated with some type of hate group. Also, in the South, where most of those crimes were committed, the justice system failed to convict those people responsible for those crimes. Usually, the judges in most of those cases were aligned with the accused, not the victim. Most of the jurors were like-minded white men with the same racist attitude directed toward black people, resulting in acquittals, hung juries, and miss trials. In some cases, the accused were never brought to justice and in other cases, decades would pass before the accused would face real justice.

Lynching of black people in the South because of Jim Crow laws was a common occurrence based on all the available information. However, what was not known at the time (or presently for that matter) was that Jim Crow laws murdered white people. I am not speaking of those white people involved in the Civil Rights Movement of the time; I am speaking of those white people who had absolutely nothing to do with the Civil Rights Movement and in most cases, supported those racist laws. This situation came about because of "The One Drop Rule".

This one rule above all else cast fear among white families and individuals in the South and even maybe throughout the United States back then. If it was discovered that a white family had African ancestry somewhere in their bloodline factually or rumored, they would have immediately become outcasts in their community. They would have been forced to move out of their all white community. Their children would have been removed from their schools and forced to attend a colored school. Plus, the One Drop Rule could have killed them, literally.

In 1965, I became an employee of Charity Hospital in

Jim Crow Did Not Exist in my Backyard

New Orleans. This was a Jim Crow, racist, segregated hospital under the command of the Catholic Church. I was hired as an operating room orderly. My duties included, but were not limited to, transporting patients to and from the operating room, decontaminating surgical instruments and supplies, gathering supplies and restocking at the end of the day and fulfilling any other duties or instructions given to me by my supervisor.

I recall on this one particular day I transported a white male patient to the operating room for surgery. I transferred the patient to the OR nurse, and I left to continue with my other duties. Approximately an hour later I heard my name being called by the nurse. I approached her, she gave me a form and instructed me to go to the blood bank and request a unit of O positive white blood. I thought nothing of her instructions about the O positive white blood as I had carried out similar instructions in the past. It was the norm at that time.

When I arrived at the blood bank, I saw the attendant sitting behind a desk doing paperwork. He seemed somewhat annoyed that I had disturbed him and he asked in an unfriendly tone what I wanted. I informed him of my instructions, and he got up from his desk and walked over to two refrigerators containing the blood packages. On the top of each refrigerator was

a sign, "White Blood" and "Colored Blood". He looked into
the refrigerator containing the white blood, pushing aside some
packages and removing others and replacing them. Then he
went to the refrigerator containing the colored blood. Finally,
he came over to me saying, tell them we are out of O positive
white blood and it will take some time before he could get
more. However, he told me to inform them that the blood bank
was well stocked with O positive colored blood.

When I return to the operating room, I motioned to the
nurse, and she joined me in the hallway. I explain to her what
the blood bank attendant instructed me to say. She looked at
me, turned and proceeded back into the operating room. A
short time later one of the doctors walked out of the OR saying
to himself in an angry voice, "I can't put nigger blood in that
white man". To this day I still recall those words.

A short time thereafter he returned to the operating room
and continued what he was doing.

I waited outside the suite, thinking the nurse would
come back to me instructing me to retrieve the colored blood.
She never did. Strange, I thought. A few days later I asked the
nurse what became of the patient. She told me he died. His
family refused the transfusion. I thought, at the time, according

to his family it was better to be white and dead than alive and colored.

Over the years, many people whose lives could have been saved were lost because of Jim Crow and that stupid rule. During World War II the United States Army was segregated. Yes, Jim Crow found its way into the ranks too. Many black soldiers died because of the fact they were denied transfusions in order to save the blood for injured white combat soldiers, and a substantial number of white soldiers died because of the One-Drop Rule. It must be remembered that most military commanders, regardless of service, held that the colored soldier or sailor was really unfit for combat duties. Therefore, the military assigned the colored soldier or sailor as laborers, stewards, truck drivers, etc. Also, most of the commanders were Southern-born with racial prejudice embedded in them before they entered the military service. It took a presidential executive order to change their behavior.

The greatest threat to the status quo, segregation, bigotry and prejudice was the mass media. Not the local media but the mass media. What the national media did in terms of civil rights, intended or unintended was to put tremendous pressure on the country's leadership to institute change. Actually, this pressure developed during the President Eisenhower/ Kennedy administrations. During the 1950's and 1960's, television was a new form of technology and entertainment in the black community. I recall my family's first television was a 24" black and white TV. With the exception of Saturday morning cartoons, it held very little interest for me. I preferred to be outside playing with my friends.

When my mother was home, she would always watch the news programs and sometimes I'd be at her side watching too. During that time period, the appearance of African Americans on TV was as frequent as Sasquatch appearing on TV today. I have always wondered how the United States maintained diplomatic relations with countries whose leaders were black or people of color because of its segregationist policies. The United Nations was still in New York, and embassies and consulates were scattered around Washington DC, Maryland and Virginia, the cradle of the Confederacy. While watching the news, sometimes the reporter would interview diplomats complaining about not being able to secure hotel rooms for themselves or their staff or being refused dining accommodations because of the color of their skin. Then, after a while, I saw or heard nothing more of it. As time went by, I found out the owners of those segregated establishments were told that if they refused to accommodate anyone because of the color of their skin, the federal government would bring pressure upon them in order for them to change their ways. It worked.

As the Civil Rights Movement began to develop, television began to play more of an important role in my life. The mass media, even the local media could no longer ignore the plight of African Americans and what we had to put up with. Actually, the Civil Rights Movement was divided into two movements. The non-violent movement headed by Dr. Martin Luther King and the attain rights by any means necessary movement headed by Mr. Malcolm X. Both appealed to me, but I was torn between the two. One side of me favored what Dr. King was preaching: love thy enemy, turn the other cheek and pray for those who despise you and say all negative things about you. The other side of me wondered how long I could take being spit upon, having eggs thrown in my face and being threatened with physical violence while singing *We shall overcome.* I wondered.

I remained non-violent, even after all of the assassinations and murders which had occurred during the period. Now that the world was being opened up to black people thanks to

[147]

the media, I can almost guarantee that the city authorities wished they would have made it illegal for black people to buy and own televisions. Prior to the development of television in the black community, we never saw blacks and whites sitting in the same restaurant, eating a meal, sitting next to each other on a city bus, or the many other things whites and blacks were engaged in together. Soon after seeing all of that we began to wonder, why not us? Why can't we do that?

The answer was clear. The reason we couldn't do those things was because we let them tell us without good reason that we couldn't. When we became aware of that fact, the Civil Rights Movement in New Orleans assumed a different identity, strength of purpose.

During my early childhood, until my family and I moved into the Desire Project, there was never any mention of Jim Crow between us kids. It existed, yet our parents sheltered us from it. I can recall traveling to the State Office Building with my mother to secure papers relating to my father's death. The line we were standing in was long; on the other hand, the line next to us only had a few people in it. I decided to move over into that line.

My mother grabbed me by the shirt collar and placed

me back in line if front of her. What I did not realize was the line I went to stand in was for whites only. Later on, she explained the facts of life to me. Soon thereafter I forgot about the whole matter. It was not that important to me because there were no restrictions on me in my neighborhood. The Desire Project was another story. From 1959 backward, Jim Crow did not exist in my backyard; Desire Project was another story. From 1959 onward his existence in my backyard became a phenomenon I had to live with.

In March of 1966, I enlisted in the United States Air Force. After I had taken the oath, I was paired up with a white enlistee. For the first time since I left my childhood neighborhood, I became friends with a white person. More importantly, I ate, slept and lived with white people. This was a new and completely different experience for me. It took some getting used to, though. However, what brought it all home was that white guy who I shared my living experience with would save my life on some distant battlefield and I would do the same for him. Jim Crow was kicked out of the backyard of the US Military almost seventy years ago. I wish I could say the same for The United States itself.

CONCLUSION

The year is 2013. African Americans have attained full and complete citizenship within the United States of America. The nation, for the first time in its history, has elected and re-elected its first African American President. Congress has established a harmonious and cordial relationship with the President, realizing that most of his agenda should pass Congress for the good of the country. Obamacare is the law of the land and is supported on both sides of the isle. Women's rights, gay rights, and everybody's rights are protected by an act of Congress. It is not a crime anymore to love who you want when you want. The Dream Act has passed, and the eleven million undocumented people have been put on the fast track to citizenship. All voter suppression laws have been deemed unconstitutional.

The President's jobs bill passed Congress overwhelmingly, and most of those Americans looking for work found jobs, thereby reducing the unemployment rate from 7.6% to 4.9% nationally and down from 13.5% to 7.5% in the African American community. Because of superstorm

Jim Crow Did Not Exist in my Backyard

Sandy, which devastated the northeastern portion of the United States, Congress, for the first time, convened a bipartisan commission to investigate climate change and make recommendations on how the country can solve this problem.

Congress has allocated billions of dollars to the nation's highway fund to repair the aging highway system and to repair or replace over 80% of deficient bridges throughout the country. I can recall portions of the Brooklyn Bridge falling into the East River a few years ago. However, that was not a surprise to New Yorkers as portions of all the bridges in New York City had fallen into the East River or the Hudson River from time to time. Realizing the importance of that issue, Congress finally acted.

On gun control, Congress had to really bite the bullet on that issue. There were so many outside groups putting pressure on Congress not to enact anything; the nation concluded that was exactly what Congress was going to do, nothing. However, when those grieving parents from Newtown, Connecticut showed up on their doorsteps several times, Congress had no choice but to act. Background checks when purchasing a gun is now the law of the land. There are more issues on the legislative agenda requiring Congress's attention however because Congress has finally put the welfare of the nation first, their approval rating along with that of the President has risen substantially.

With the exception of the election of President Obama and Obamacare being the law of the land, all of the above statements are untrue and absolutely false. I believe that there is one reason and one reason only why the President and his policies are treated with such vile disdain in Congress. Two words: Jim Crow. Jim Crow died a few years ago, and now his son is trying to resurrect his father's racist, bigoted policies. No matter how you shape it, look at it or feel about it, it's all reduced to its lowest possible denominator, RACE. Those white men in congress cannot bear the fact that a black man is in power and calling the shots. They cannot rationalize how the country came to such a fate. Well, there is a simple answer, Vote. For the first time in the nation's history, the minority population cast more votes than the white population. Also, in 2012, for the first time in the nation's history, there were more minority babies born in the country than white babies. This fact is setting up the country for a complete change in the political power structure. The Republicans, especially those on the far and extreme right, have decided to use the tactics of Jim Crow and his son.

Many of those in the Tea Party and other extreme groups have portrayed the President as a savage, running around the jungle with a bone in his nose, carrying a spear and wearing a grass skirt. There were cartoon drawings in newspapers all over the country portraying the president and his wife as terrorists. He dressed in Arab clothing, and she dressed in military style clothing with a weapon slung over her back doing a fist pump. A potent Jim Crow tactic. Back in the day those very same people only under a different name portrayed black people as shiftless with big lips, big white eyes and chasing after white women, for example, "The Birth of a Nation". The strategy worked back then. Some believe it could work now. Take away the President's humanity in order for him to appear as not being one of us, instead the peace-loving, God-fearing, law-abiding white folks of the United States.

Another tactic used by some US congressmen and others was an attempt to delegitimize him by claiming he is not the legitimate President of The United States because he was not born in the US. They circulated rumors that he was born in Kenya. This came to be known as the Birther movement. It is a

[153]

fact that the 2008 Republican presidential candidate, Senator John McCain, was not born in the United States. However, there was no outcry by the Birthers and some congressmen for him to produce his birth certificate. Why I wonder? The 2012 Republican candidate for president, Gov. Mitt Romney, was born in a family of polygamists. Polygamy in the United States was illegal, and in order to escape criminal prosecution for violating that law, the family relocated to Mexico. During the Mexican Revolution, the families were forced to relocate back to the United States. Just think of the impact that would have had on President Obama's political chances to be elected president if that situation occurred in his family. Based on his past family issues regarding his birth and place of birth, the outcry from the extreme conservative right would have been so loud I do not know if Mr. Obama could have survived politically. Yet, in Mr. Romney's case, there was hardly a whimper expressed by the conservative right. Why, because he is a white man. These are just a few of the Jim Crow tactics being used against the President. There are many more.

According to Senator Mitch McConnell, the Senator Minority Leader, a very powerful man in Congress, his first priority was not to the nation's business as his oath of office required, but to make sure that President Obama was "A one-term president". His first priority did not work, and he has paid a political price for making such a statement.

The Dream Act supported by the majority of Republicans in congress at the time removed their support when it was learned that President Obama supported the bill too. Senator Marco Rubio, Republican from Florida, decided not to support the very bill he sponsored because of the President's support. President Obama endorsed a pathway to citizenship for the eleven million undocumented persons in the country. Yet there were those in the Republican Party advocating self-deportation or not supporting a pathway to citizenship, claiming it was amnesty. However, in the past, they supported such a bill.

Voter suppression and nullification, it seems like I heard of that somewhere before, in the Jim Crow South maybe. With the re-election of President Obama and the overwhelming support he received from the minority community, the Republican Party found itself in an untenable position. That is, losing the majority of national elections. The decision was made that if an election cannot be won fairly, cheat. They made it difficult or in some cases impossible for minorities to register to

[155]

vote and vote overwhelming support from Republican Party members throughout the country. Also, a poll tax and literacy test were instituted which directly affected elderly black voters. However, the ploy did not work, due to the fact that black voters hunted high and low for the necessary documents in order to register and waited in long lines for up to eight hours in order to vote. During the height of the Civil Rights Movement, we were taught never to take our eyes off the prize. That was true then, and it is vital now.

It cannot be stressed more forcefully that the power of the vote is the ultimate expression of the will of the American people. Yet, many politicians have come to the conclusion that their personal agenda trumps the nation's business and gun control is a vital aspect of the nation's business with over 90% of the American people supporting some type of a gun control measure. Since the Newtown shooting in December 2012, over 5,000 Americans have been killed with a gun and the number is going up daily. According to most Republican congressmen and all extreme right wing talk show hosts, they know who they are, President Obama wants to declare the Second Amendment as being null and void, and he wants to take away all your guns.

Jim Crow Did Not Exist in my Backyard

Under the leadership of the previous white presidents, gun control measures were enacted and were stricter than what President Obama proposes, yet there was very little dissent at that time. All politicians know that an election cannot be won without money and lots of it. The National Rifle Association has declared if any conservative politician supports any type of gun control measure, they would lose all funding from the NRA. It worked. No gun control measure has made it to the floor of the House of Representatives for a vote now nor will it the future, and none ever will as long as President Obama is the Chief Executive. Maybe the next president can get some movement on this and other issues provided he is not black.

In spite of all the setbacks handed to the President by the Jim Crow Congress, the economic vitality of the country has improved tremendously since the devastating economic crash of 2008. History will judge this President as one of the greatest presidents this country has ever produced. He ended the Iraq war, a war we should have never started and is ending the Afghanistan war, a war we should have pursued from the very beginning as a result of 9/11. He brought Osama Bin Laden to justice, something no other previous president could do. The housing market is up, and foreclosures are down. The stock market is up compared to where it was only a few years ago, below 7000. Obamacare is working in spite of the Republican Congressmen attempts to repeal it thirty-eight times. Plus, the President is a likable guy, someone you would like to have a beer with.

The true measure of a nation is determined by the will and consent of those being governed. The United States of America is the most powerful nation in the world, and that power emanates from the consent of the people through their elected officials. When those elected officials violate the power and the trust bestowed upon them by the American people, then they should be held accountable. Congress has failed to live up to its creed, "Government of the people, By the people. For the people," and because of its failure the country is on the verge of becoming a racially-centered nation. The United States will always have racial differences to deal with; that is the nature of being a democracy. However, those differences should not reach the level of hatred, bigotry, and mistrust as professed by Jim Crow. What has been lost within the conscious of these United States is, we will all prosper together, or we will all fail together, there's no other choice.

There will never be a condition within the United States

whereby racism will be eliminated henceforth and forever-more. It just will not happen. On the other hand, that is not to say that we cannot live in peace and harmony with our neigh-bor, realizing we all fall short of the grace of God. No man can label another man as being not entirely human or 3/5 human without indemnifying himself. The human race evolves from the same gene pool. However, there are those in this country who will try to maintain the status quo ensuring an everlasting place for racism to exist in these United States of America.